Acclaim for
FALLING AWAKE

"Sometimes funny, sometimes sad, often insightful, but always poignant, Mary Lou Sanelli's essays take her readers on marvelous journeys of the spirit. With a style that other writers envy, she puts together words in a unique way that inspires the reader to pause, to think and, ultimately, to smile. Whether it's about the whimsical characters in her family or the capricious activities of her friends, Mary Lou's writing is comfortable and personal, and completely unforgettable."

— Jill Buhler, Editor in Chief, *Peninsula Lifestyle magazine*

"Sanelli has her feet on the ground and her every sense attuned to the changing seasons of planet and populace alike."

— Richard T. Jameson, *Queen Anne News*

"Mary Lou Sanelli creates a uniquely wise, witty and assuming voice. In it she captures not only her own heart but her readers' hearts as well."

— John Brewer, editor and publisher, *Peninsula Daily News*

"Mary Lou Sanelli's weekly commentary is bright, incisive and insightful."

— Ed Bremer, *KSER FM*

"Today's column had me giggling out loud as I drank my morning coffee. I just love her insights. She gets to the core of things I can relate to much more than Dave Barry (as funny as he is!). So, from one faithful reader, my kudos and appreciation."

— Rhonda Curry, Founder, Girlfriends' Bookclub

FALLING AWAKE

By the same author:

FALLING AWAKE

AN AMERICAN WOMAN GETS A GRIP
ON THE WHOLE CHANGING WORLD

ONE ESSAY AT A TIME

MARY LOU SANELLI

An Aequitas Book
Pleasure Boat Studio: A Literary Press
New York

Sanelli, Mary Lou
Falling Awake: An American Woman Gets A Grip
On The Whole Changing World, One Essay At A Time

ISBN: 978-1-929355-38-9
FIRST PRINTING
Library of Congress Control Number: 2006937248

Cover Image: Way Past Midnight by Lois Silver.
Courtesy of the Lisa Harris Gallery, Seattle, WA.
Painting of author by Pam Berglundh.
Book Design by Diane Rigoli, Rigoli Artstudio, San Francisco,
www.rigoliartstudio.com.

Aequitas Books
About the Press: Aequitas Books is a new imprint of Pleasure Boat Studio: A Literary Press. We are located in New York City. The new imprint focuses on sociological and philosophical themes in non-fiction. Pleasure Boat Studio books are carried by Baker & Taylor, Ingram, Partners/West, Brodart, and Small Press Distribution (SPD).

For more information,

Pleasure Boat Studio: A Literary Press
201 West 89 Street, New York, NY 10024
Email: pleasboat@nyc.rr.com
Tel: 212-362-8563   Fax: 888-810-5308
URL: www.pleasureboatstudio.com

PRINTED IN CANADA

by Hignell Book Printing

Aequitas Books is a proud subscriber to the Green Press Initiative. This program encourages the use of 100% post-consumer recycled paper with environmentally friendly inks for all printing projects in an effort to reduce the book industry's economic and social impact. With the cooperation of Hignell Book Printing Company, we are pleased to offer this book as a Green Press book.

ACKNOWLEDGMENTS:

These essays are a collection of writings that began as commentaries and columns, aired and/or published since September 11, 2001, on *Weekday, KUOW: Northwest Public Radio*; *Weekend Edition: NPR*; *The Seattle Times*; *Art Access*; *Peninsula Lifestyle Magazine*; *The Port Townsend and Jefferson County Leader*; *The Peninsula Daily News*; *The Queen Anne News*; *The Magnolia News*; *The Belltown Messenger*; *The Belltown Paper*; *Northwest Palate Magazine*; *Northwest AMP Magazine*; *Northwest Woman Magazine*; *Northwest Women's Outdoor Magazine*; *Raven Chronicles*; *Go World Travel Magazine*; KSER FM; KONP AM; and KBCS FM.

I wish to thank the Fundacion Varipariso Artists Residency in Spain, where these essays were compiled and finished.

As always, I owe an enormous amount of gratitude to my publisher, Jack Estes. I will never cease to appreciate, or fail to live up to your faith in me.

I thank Sara Muirhead who patiently helped to edit this manuscript. She is a writer's best vision of an editor.

And I wish to thank my women friends, especially Jeane Myers, who continued to give me confidence boosts through the humbling process of making an idea of a book into a reality. We are friends in the best sense, nudging each other to take risks. And reminding each other that doing is everything.

For Larry, who always encourages me to take the necessary risks for what I believe in.

CONTENTS

VII.

... a man who looked inward and showed me how to do the same,
which has pretty much been the aim of my writing ever since.
— page 179

Polite and blind we live.

— Lillian Hellman (1906 - 1984)

AUTHOR'S INTRODUCTION: FALLING AWAKE

Like a lot of writers, I was unable to focus in the immediate aftermath of September 11, 2001. Why bother, I thought, as I'd never be able to make sense of such chaos. Chaos that has riddled other countries for years, but I suppose it's human nature to be motivated most when the world's dangers befall your our own back yard.

But after only a few hours, with a deep and horrible fear throughout my entire body, I did start to write, not only because it's the only way I know how to push through to what worries me most, but I focus best in front of a computer screen. What modern writer doesn't? I sat, wished myself luck, and started in. And for weeks after, nothing else, short of holding my husband a little closer at night, seemed to offer any comfort from the doom suspended like fog over the whole changing world.

Actually, the opening essay was written in such an anxious state that, given the usual uncreative nature of my worry, fretting-through-my-finger-tips turned out to be an illuminating, productive relief. I suppose even in a time of crisis nothing is more exhilarating than the thought of accomplishment.

Then something I never expected: While listening to Seattle's Northwest Public Radio program, *Weekday*, I heard the producer ask for written responses to the disaster. I called the station.

To my surprise (I actually gasped into the receiver), the producer answered the phone. "Well, um ... I've written something," I said. "Read it to me," he replied. "Right now?" I asked, startled by the briskness of the request. I confess I knew nothing, then, of the immediateness of the newsroom. "That's what I said," he responded, but with a willingness to instruct rather than impatience, which was to be responsible for much of what understanding I now have of the radio medium we both love. Oooo-kay, I thought, as I sank to the floor and read my piece aloud with all the vehemence within me.

But beneath the intensity, I was curious as to whether he'd want to hear what I had to say. My writing is more likely to respond to the personal, everyday experience than to any worldly assessment, not always easy to market within the media formula where only "experts" are supposed to deliver an opinion. And only in their field of "expertise."

Yet, to my surprise, the most incredible thing happened: I was invited into the studio. Which led to writing and airing ten such grounding examinations in the next year and a half, essays that allowed me to see clear through to the center of what exactly had happened on September 11. And what had not.

Now I look back at these writings and one thing becomes especially clear: They were never meant to explain but to explore. Allowed the rare freedom to mull over the disaster my own way made me so certain I'd found my calling I remember thinking that if there is felicity in the world this was surely its gift to me. I walked around looking happy because I was happy, numb to any emotion other than pleased.

Through the eighteen months that followed, I came to realize how any writing is unavoidably defined by its exposure to the world. As the media sought to poise life for listeners tiring of fear, fumbling for stories that would secure an audience, the unrelenting anxiousness eased for most Americans. Spirits lifted, life renewed. Commentaries such as mine were cancelled.

At a personal level, I knew my work needed to move on to another phase of growth or suffer under the weight of redundancy, which is a blight to the life of any writer. And no work is without its depressions. We have no choice but to move beyond the ones we can no longer fill, and focus on the ones we can.

And once I established in my own mind that I was, indeed, legitimate even if I wasn't writing strictly about news matters, that it was large work to write about the small things, and serious work to write with humor, I was entirely relieved to do so, resulting in stories about my home town of Port Townsend, Washington, and home city of Seattle, natural to a writer who, for over a decade, has divided her life and work between two dwellings: a 500-square-foot cottage that sits squarely in the center of a small-town garden, and an even smaller condo lodged within the verticalness of downtown, high rise living. A straddling of two utterly different worlds and mind-sets.

And I began to write about family dynamics. And traveling, which I love to do, and my garden, which I also love, and how it suffers because I love to travel more. Subjects written not only to keep up with my new work as a print and radio columnist, where often I'm not asked nor allowed to be as political as I'd like to be, but also as an alleviative to the politics that seemed to be spinning rapidly out of control and difficult to be on top of unless that is all you want to think, talk, and write about.

Today I fear parts of this collection, by publication time, will be regarded as out of date. Mostly because, to Americans in particular, anything not of a daily spin can seem immediately passé. Consider, though, the time it takes to write, publish, and distribute a book. All of which makes it, by its very nature, last year's news, the writer unable to build the present into its pages any more than a contractor can build a home into a house.

Yet, books distinguish literature from the day-to-day grind of journalism, and when I think of the most unique columns and essays, I don't care what the writing is about; it's the insight I remember, not the timeliness. Good writing boils down to simple stories well told.

And one of the things I love most about this collection of short essays is that though they are dated, you can read them in any order, and in a few minutes you're finished. After which you can place your page marker between brainstorms and fall into sleep.

Still, there will be those who prefer over-analyzing or a more journalistic approach to the intimacy I like to slide into my work. I'll likely endure a bit of rejection from that realm.

Because, having had my fill of writing journalism with a short stint at a major Seattle newspaper, and with all due respect to the genre, I find it dull not to reveal something right up through the middle of a story. It was an experimental phase before I found the courage to admit there is a wide difference between what sounds good as far as writing commitments go, and what is good as far as writing commitments go. Before I was willing to trade prestige for peace of mind. I admire good objective writing, but I rarely envy it. And envy is an excellent guiding compass. It helps a writer decide between what she thinks she should be writing and what it is she really wants to write.

To me, a good essay's readability relies on the comforting presence of the writer, it's much like a lively exchange between people. And yet this conversational style is often resisted by those with an impartial preference. A preference that is "fact based," as one of my editors likes to say, but that lacks a certain human quality: The why of who we are and why we think the things we do. It saddens me that more editors, publishers, and radio programmers don't recognize that a sincere quest to understand one's place in the world is not self-indulgence but the very access many readers and listeners are looking for. Nothing is more satisfying than connecting to what matters in the mind of another. I write to connect: others to others, others to me, me to me. These are good fits.

Of course, the gender divide on this issue is vast.

It was impossible for me, in the beginning, to imagine this collection. But here it is, compiled, bound, and out the door. Sort of. In private, I still sit up in the middle of the night with the same doubts some of these essays arouse because there is nothing quite as sobering as falling awake as you light upon the cruel realities of the world. What began one fearful day not so many years ago as a response to a catastrophe has gradually, fed by time, led directly back to the one question I sat with initially: Is there any possibility that maybe, just maybe, there is peace to be had in our world?

In ten years time, I want to be able to open this book and announce that we have come far since that horrible time when everything was shaky for everybody. And yet, by the time of publication, it will seem like eons since Cindy Sheehan, a zillion times braver than the man she demanded to see, pitched her tent outside of the Crawford Ranch so that she might look into the eyes of an evangelical president and ask the question I ask myself every day: Toward what betterment is all this war for? While the man who refuses to see her sidesteps the question, forcing millions unlucky enough to be caught in the crossfire to accept their fate.

So, sadly, my guess is that these will remain impossible words for me to say.

But not to imagine.

And don't ask how I'll turn imagination into a lifeline. I just will.

I.

"I feel like a fool. All those years of Sunday school, and still the apocalypse catches me off guard."

— Sarah Vowell

UP FOR GRABS

September 11, 2001

After my husband leaves for work, I am well into my second round of sleep, bed all mine for another hour, when the phone rings.

Without his usual warmth of greeting, which causes me to flinch and sit up because I *know* when my husband's tone is set by fear, he tells me that it's a dark and frightening day in our country. Straight away I think our president has been shot and, I'm both startled and completely unsurprised, my mouth forming an oval of disbelief while my insides register the news with ease.

But he says, "No, turn on the TV." So I do.

Later in the day, under a cloudless sky, I ride my bicycle to the summit of town sluggishly, as if pushing my weight through sea. My routine of Motown-on-headphones as I pump up the hill would be inappropriate today, but the pure act of riding feels acceptable, the habit of me refusing to withdraw entirely.

Midway up Morgan Hill, the summit of Port Townsend, a woman I know by sight but not by name (which is pretty much how I know most of the community) is weeding her garden, and I stop because I need to connect with someone,

2

anyone, realizing, perhaps for the first time with such clarity, how utterly together in all of this we really are. But when she asks me to meditate with her, to send out positive vibes to the universe, I experience a total *dis*connect, and though I'm not proud to admit this, I want to slap her upside the head. Why the word "vibes" used in this context on this particular day sets me off, I don't know. It just does. And as I ride away, it's liberating to mull on what my honest answer should have been, revving my courage with a slew of comebacks.

And when I come to the peak where the Pacific reaches clear out to the Gulf Islands of Canada, I see only, or rather can *focus* on only, a woman polishing her lipstick-red Mercedes. Though I know people do and say stupid things when under stress, her action is a splinter I can't dislodge. "Show some respect!" I shout. I have bypassed the religion of my Italian birthright, but when irritated to the point of anger I home right in on the attitude. No self-censoring. Entirely incredulous. Even if I suffer in the guilty aftermath of who it can reduce me to.

Finally, connected by phone to my dad on the shoreline of Connecticut, safe and sound, he says he can see the plumes of smoke and that my sister walked home from work with thousands of others, across the Brooklyn Bridge, never knowing she *could* leg it from lower Manhattan to Flatbush Avenue.

Then, in the voice he uses when he's about to plow through the small talk, he says, "Mussolini was a fanatic, too, and the only way to stop him was to fight fire with fire. You can't reason with crazy people!" He says all this in what I call his Godfather voice, the one signaling that the subject, which is really his ruling, is closed to argument. And though I won't repeat his judgement with some (most) of my friends, on this calendar day I agree with him. I don't play the optimist with my dad. He's seen too much of war for that.

Explode. Crumble. Burn. As the shock of Manhattan's twin towers fall for the hundredth time on the TV screen, who knows why I sit, stunned and horrified, instead of turning off the set, or why I think of the cows I saw yesterday while I bicycled on Whidbey Island. I suppose the mind makes its own way into coping. Anyhow, one cow mooed and mooed alone by the fence, so I stopped to ask the farmer why?

"She needs a bull is all, eh-yup, she wants to mate."

And in the midst of today's horror that divides a baby boomer's past from all there is to come, I find the simple desirous act of nature and sound coming from the cave of that cow a small comfort while I watch a new war, fraught with so many old ones, unfold, every ordinary thing about life seeming up for grabs as I write this, because it would be cowardly to write about anything else.

EACH RELYING ON THE OTHER
September 2001

One day short of a week after the World Trade Center came crumbling down, my friend Rachel and I are ready to conquer the small details of life again.

And so we wait with dozens of other commuters to board the Bainbridge Island ferry that will land us in the hub of Seattle. That is, just before a bomb scare is announced over the loud-speaker.

Oddly, no one seems to believe the threat is real or think much at all about the relevance of an imminent explosive device as we compare appointments we'll be late for, schedules we cannot keep. For now, an air of alliance still surrounds, a need to get along oh-so-well.

So, while canines sniff out the peril, I think of my phone conversation last night with Deanna, an old college chum, an editorial of straightforwardness. Fecklessly, she blames men for the bombings which, in a grappling-sort-of-way, helps us both to cope. In a nasally Brooklyn accent I can't even begin to imitate she said, "What did *they* expect from a man who makes movies of men training to kill us?" And I agreed with her vague group of "they" that we accuse whenever we can't take responsibility or need a scapegoat because I wanted to commiserate about something now that we no longer share a dorm room or *any*thing other than history.

At present, we arrive in the city, an hour later than expected, no bomb found, trying to behave our way back to normal day-to-day, so, um, we go shopping. And not because our foolish president thinks we should do our part to help a lagging economy but because I'm human, which means I'm really good at finding others like myself. Rachel and I move at the same pace through the aisles, through *life*, and the in-the-moment endeavor of retail browsing distracts our minds from the worry we carry.

In the GAP we try on jeans, perform a cheesy little booty dance as we pose like models a hundred years younger than we, luxuriate in a day of diversion in spite of the world's edginess, her son pouting at home, our work, husbands, a zillion obligations, and fidgety hormones.

In the stall beside us, a woman says to *her* friend, "Damn, if we send all our boys off to war, even if I loss twenty pounds off my butt, there won't be no boys left in the city to date."

At this, Rachel and I laugh. At ourselves in the mirror, yes, but mostly because it is such a relief to do so again, the weighty air of dread dissipating as I fall to my knees, pure gratitude coming over me, the kind that makes me feel more alive. And that's exactly what I need to feel: gratefulness for this friendship, that my family is safe, my life intact. Not Catholic-born guilt over the fact that when the sky fell over New York, I slept peacefully, my cat a fur-ball in my curve.

At some point in all this, hunger wedges in. So on we walk to Westlake Center, Seattle's first mall-within-downtown. And at the food court, where Mediterranean chop-chop salads await like some wonderful holy things, I tell Rachel what another confidant, Jane, told me just yesterday when my vulnerabilities felt more shaky than ever: Remember, dear, EVIL is LIVE spelled backwards.

Silly words, Lord knows. And yet I hold to them much as I hold to this plastic tray and make my way through Seattle's lunch-hour crowd. With both hands. Each relying on the other.

Because that's how it works. Reassurance comes in subtle ways.

FLAGS AND FAITH

October 2001

How can I begin to explain to my next-door neighbor who asks if I'll display an image of an American flag photocopied on his printer that I *am* patriotic, but a flag in my living room window, well, ah ...

Every part of me shudders because I know his allegiance is set in stone and there's no way to convey what my patriotic gestures are, if there are any, which, in my flag-less yard, car, and lapel, clearly there are not. It's as if my excuses fade before my eyes into bubbles of air, our differences circling each other like wrestlers on the mat. I simply lose the oomph to explain myself.

My neighbor is a forty-year-old man who lives with his mother in the home where he was born. A man who fishes and hunts and brings me slabs of salmon so fresh and moist I am drenched in gratitude. Yet as he walks from my yard, laminated flag in his hand, I know it will be awhile before his generosity returns. But that's all right. In these disconnected times, I appreciate a man who looks after his neighbors, who loves his community even if he flat out dislikes most of the newcomers in it.

Truth is, I've never searched this far into my feelings on flags before. So, desperate for an ear to bend, I call my husband to express every thought that enters my mind. And though he says, "Hon, I'm in a meeting, can I call you back?" I am caffeine-induced by now and can't help myself from blurting out that flags, to me, are a lot like God and I'm sorry but I can't find any solace in that icon either—not as I find in my garden or anyone's garden and last night looking up at the moon in a sky so clear and flecked with stars now *that* was a totally divine experience for me but if I fold my fists and try to pray I can't wring any truth out of it and that's the same empty feeling I get when I look at our flag because lately it hasn't lived up to the admirable things it's supposed to stand for, you know? Larry, you *know*?"

"Jesus," I say, exhaling, knowing it's my fault he's hung up and that the world is no longer a place I know very well. I rinse out my coffee mug and head out the door for my commute to the city.

All of the cars waiting to cross over the Hood Canal Bridge are slowed to a crawl. It startles me how a police officer is peering suspiciously into each. I sort of appreciate his effort to protect. No, actually I don't. And as I pass over the span of steel, the sun rising warm and white behind me, I fear how he will evaluate *me*? My heartbeat quickens. Inside my head, I hear a scold: *Hey you! Your jeans are too tight, shoes too pointy, and, damn girl, turn down that dance music!* And the most frightening thing happens: I reach for the dial to obey.

All right. So maybe the rest of the world has gone crazy. This is what I think just before threatening myself to turn up the music again. And when I drive off the bridge, Beyonce is singing so loudly from the cave of my car that one of the road workers gives a thumbs up, and I begin to breathe fully from my diaphragm again.

Most people piling off the Bainbridge Island ferry are headed for work, but I head straight for the Seattle Art Museum to see the Annie Liebowitz portraits, where famous women look down at me from photographs that are a bit grand and showy for my taste, perfect for someone who prefers an opera at Benaroya to a concert at Bumbershoot. Still, I'm struck by the fact that each reminds me, with a presence that might as well speak, that it is not the women of this world who are responsible for the trouble we are in. Nor is it we who will retaliate with presidential-size will and power.

Yet it will need to be us who collectively raise our brushes to sweep with panoptic strokes the humanity back into this bleak picture. For aren't we always the ones who clean up the mess men leave behind?

And then the portrait of the artist's mother expands into view. She is the reason I am here, I decide. Her genuineness opens perfectly visible, her tenacity nearly possible to touch.

Her image is what I leave with as I walk outside past the towering, flat-headed man who pounds, *pounds* it into me that I'm less than life-size in his shadow. Still, for the first time since last month, when Enormous Fear set in, I am one huge possibility in his wake. And though some would regard this as ego, I know it is courage. The kind that can lie dormant and then, at a single moment, flare up to set me into action.

BACK AT THE AIRPORT
October 2001

Last month, resolution was an easy vow: I am not flying. Anywhere. Not a decision I needed to mull over.

But fall has descended, work pressures escalate, and the impending holiday season is a Chihuahua at my heels, nipping me toward panic so that the thought of not being able to escape to where my husband and I might actually wake, eat, and sleep on the same schedule, well, I weigh this against the possibility of our lives falling from the sky and here we are at the airport, the lines at the screening checkpoint as long as the list of reasons why we travel.

In a culture that practices competition over conciliation, as ours mostly does, the airport screening line is, for now, an exemplary model of patience and appeasement. Good behavior is everywhere with a shrug and a smile.

The important thing to remember, I tell myself, is not to question the efficiency of all this security *aloud* while moving slowly forward and to cleanse my handbag of all weapons: Tweezers, tiny screwdriver for my sunglasses, and forget about that chopstick to clasp my hair back. No belt, jewelry or under-wire bra. Fortunately, the result is, whew, I pass under the screening arch silently. Feeling triumphant, I look back to see an elderly, respectable woman (gray suit, hair in a bun, *nylons*) straddling her legs while a man half her age sweeps her body with a foot- long, baton-like scanner. The look on her face: utter humiliation.

I think this might always be the account readers think I made up for an unwonted story, but I swear to you and to my producer at KUOW that just after I take a seat at the gate and shuffle through my purse for a lipstick, I'm stunned by what my fingers find: full-size, solid steel scissors that have been in my bag since July when it was still possible to hem a skirt en route to San Francisco. For a moment I want to turn them in, but considering that scenario scares it right out of me again. Besides, I love these scissors. They were my mother's scissors. That is before I stole them. I close my bag and chat up the woman beside me, because whenever I'm seriously nervous I can't talk calmly enough while my inner voice is screeching so loud a dog's ears would flop back.

Done. Decision made. I'll be keeping the scissors.

Later, after boarding, it's easy to forget how much the world of flying has changed as I, five feet two, a hundred-ten pounds, try to bench-press a carry-on into the overhead compartment while the six-foot, beefed-up guy behind ignores my effort. And as I stare into a mindless magazine hoping the salesman on my left will stop trying to acquaint himself, and the ma'am on my right won't bring out photos of the grand kids.

But here's where familiarity abruptly shifts: When I order a glass of wine to expedite leaving real life behind, the stewardess apologizes for the quality she serves (twist-off!), because she can no longer carry a corkscrew. For some reason I feel smug about my covert scissors, fake nonchalance, go back to my sandwich and grapes, sans knife or fork.

So much depends on this flight. A whole nation struggles to nick the image of airplane-as-bomb.

Soon as we touch down, I burst into tears. The desert sky is radiant, air mid-seventies. In two hours and ten minutes, Seattle's chilly gray is a memory and I'm in the bright blue eye of a warm afternoon.

For all of us braving the skies for the first time since September, what better time to appreciate how travel is not a given but a luxury, and the way we do so, like everything else, is colored by the past. Nothing will take the edge off this experience for years to come, if ever.

Remembering helps, too: When I was eight, I had to recite a few lines in a play: *What's new in the zoo? What's new in the zoo. Oh, I saw a snake comb his hair with a rake, that's what's new in the zoo.* And I still recall how wonderful it felt to finally deliver those words, the stress of achievement behind me. It's the kind of small feat I accomplished today. With the same sigh of relief wound around it.

PONDERING THIS WAR
AT DAWN

October 2001

It is impossible to sleep when you're afraid. All you can do is think. Any fear I refused to acknowledge by day defines my life by night, echoing out a hollow where worry collects. If I try to ignore it, it amplifies until there is no room left for anything related to reason.

Here I lie, a woman whose hands are resting on her stomach, eyes open, waiting out the hours because I am less afraid of terrorism than of this say-so war on terrorism, of the depression it is causing in me both tangibly and spiritually.

How would I fill in the blank on a national identity card calling for my religion, what word would I use to describe a faith in living with one man and two cats on half a city lot in a cottage built to nurture? How would I explain that a small office overlooking a haphazard garden is my temple, writing my religion because it gives definition to every thing truthful I believe in.

A silence falls, and the moon appears so white it glows like china between the clouds. How can it be that while we lob tank shells over women and children in Afghanistan, from the warmth of my bed there is still so much beauty in the world? I'm exhausted with the effort it takes to ponder this, so to spare myself, I think about trivial things, day-to-day things: how a younger friend tries on my knowledge like clothes, how it leaves me guarded, afraid to straight talk from a candid place gathered like weight with the years. Yet with older friends I recoil, come up short of experience, weigh in a little naive. Especially on most issues concerning the Mideast and its myriad of wars.

I roll over. My husband and I lie protected as seeds in warm bread. We are in the truest, most literal sense, connected.

Shouldn't I bask in this luxury? Why this knot of dread growing?

And how can I assert my view of war, an opinion I have to make up as I go? Because it does alter. Easily and frequently. For instance, last night I attended a production of "The Vagina Monologues," where I was told that 400,000 women were raped in this country last year alone. Right then I revised my belief into this: *Women have been at war all along.*

I take my husband's hand, clutch it in two of mine and wonder if others lie in their beds looking up through a pane of glass, war experience nil but still wanting, as I do, out of revenge and retaliation, out of the shame both instill. And, yet, how can we *not* examine our part in this from all angles as an X-ray scans from the outside in?

Maybe it's not so bad, in terms of war, to be uncertain, other than knowing how utterly appalling war is in every real and imaginable way. Perhaps by not being convinced of anything political, I leave space for little brain waves of meaning to trickle in.

Meaning is not trickling in.

15

I try to let go of the issues if for no other reason than to lift myself out from under what feels like a burden of failure. As the sun begins to rise, I wear down. Sleep nudges in.

One last question as I cling to sympathy for and abhorrence of those who accept war as an alternative: In the midst of all the wars men seem hell bent on waging and prolonging, can a woman find a calm within?

My promise is to try.

IN THE MAIL
November 2001

There is an unspoken, golden rule between a woman writer and a mailman who sees her five times a week sitting at her desk in her bathrobe, hair uncombed, approachable as fallout: He must never tell anyone what she looks like at half past nine in the morning when he slips her mail through the slot in her office door.

Usually he releases the envelopes so that they plop to the floor in a heap, but this time he knocks because, times what they are mail-wise, he has to hand me the oily mess addressed from my mother and looking like some green thing sprung from another planet.

"Yes, indeed," he says, assuring this would be the package stopping the flow of mail through our post office had the carriers not surrounded it, nodding in agreement, because they know a bundle just like it has been mailed to my home once a month, summer through fall, for the past decade. And though they've been instructed to destroy any mail as suspect as mine, mail that leaks memories of my childhood in the form of olive oil and garlic, in this instance they can't help being likeable men instead of mail police.

The package contains my mother's homemade pesto. She sends me a jar of it every time she thins her basil, and by the time it arrives on this coast, it has oozed into a cardboard box softened out of form, delivered to me in a white plastic mail bucket growing greener as we stare at it.

Like so many who have adopted the Northwest as their own, I've moved away from family. In my absence, my mother longs to be needed. So she sends the sumptuous in the mail and I'm indebted to any postal worker willing to make the call that the vowel at the end of my name likely means food in the mail and not anthrax. And that the problem with my mother's packaging is not really a *problem* other than the mess it makes.

This morning, along with the pesto, something else menacing came in the mail, one of those envelopes where the look of it stings you somewhere deep in your solar plexus. It's from the landlord who owns the building that houses my dance studio downtown, where our city's funky charm is disappearing the fastest, gasping for breath, renovation pulling round it like a noose. Apparently, my rent is going up again, which I already know because the rumor swept through the building, tenant-to-tenant, like the kind of fire you build with the cedar shingles torn off a dilapidated roof.

The letter formally states that the rent increase is due to 911, and it keeps stating 911: "911 will cause insurance rates to skyrocket." "911 will make it difficult to do business." I've been doing my world-news-homework yet I have no clue as to what this number, used in this particular context, means. Some measure on a ballot? Or did someone dial the three digits to report his building is in violation of a building code (or forty/fifty building codes)? Then, it hits me: We've already abbreviated September Eleventh. Which isn't a major catastrophe in the larger picture, but still, God, it makes me see red.

Mad as hell, I want to march right down to my landlord's office to demand he not Xmas the emotion out of a day that deserves to be spelled out in full, spoken in absolute presence of mind, syllable by syllable as if sacred text. I *want* to, but I don't.

Instead, I read a magazine to calm myself only to learn that for each year of peace in our world there have been 400 of war. I let the pages fall to the floor and head straight to the kitchen to stick my spoon into my jar of pesto. In the wake of such a statistic, I will make a pig of myself.

Thank goodness for the mail as we still know it. And for my home set in the middle of half a city lot, where the postman still walks clear up to my door without fear. Because of him, I have restored faith, oh not in politicians, that's more than I can pretend. But in our world, in its people more alike than different, what I had so much of before the world changed in the space of a fall day.

And though I can't eat food as rich as pesto every day, I'm sort of married to a low-fat, no-fun diet, I'm grateful that for a few dollars of postage, I can still count on it for a fling.

A CITY LIKE NO OTHER

June 2002

I thought I'd stayed away too long, that if I once knew how to be in Manhattan, the time had passed.

But after leaving JFK and weaving through Queens in a taxi vying for speed points, I find my footing again in a city that reeks of a zillion past lives plus my own. And from this point on, I'm so far on the other side of estrangement I'm at home again: I enter my favorite diner, order a bagel with a smear, smile when I'm called sweetheart by a waiter I *recognize*.

I am, and always have been, both thrilled and repelled by the constant, buzzing life of this city; in awe of its tolerant sidewalks that bind millions together while, at the same time, bias keeps them apart. And while the names of certain neighborhoods have changed, their effect on me is the same.

Here's what I see: Rumors that the city is cleaner and "safer" than a decade ago are true. Parks are alive again with people from the neighborhood instead of the indigent, not a prostitute to be seen even in Times Square. What *became* of all the disadvantaged is the question no one wants to answer. I'm guessing they've been squeezed north of 115th Street, where tourist maps halt as if the city falls into the Hudson north of

Central Park. But that's another story, and I've returned to relish rather than scrutinize. Mostly because I don't want to be guilt-ridden the entire time, carrying around the burden of remorse when everyone else on the street seems to be handling history just fine.

After staring at red, blue, and green veins of subway line, it takes me awhile to remember it's the A train, north to south, that runs to the site of the World Trade Center.

On the train eight men wear work boots stained with a fine, white ash as if they've just walked through the remains of a bonfire. And like the tourist I am, I want to point out my observation but realize New Yorkers, by now, are Zen-like about the commute downtown. They sit side by side with the construction crew, climb to street level with the construction crew, without a word passed between them.

Everyone describes the site, so I won't, except to say that it is as hollow as they write. And because there isn't anything new to say about the sixteen acres of grave I stare into, I focus on the sound, how jack-hammers seem to fill the air with rage. Then I turn to the outside of the emptiness: a deli and hair salon boarded up, surrounding buildings wrapped in black mesh as if prayer shawls drape their pain.

And while it is one thing to hear about this site, or view it via satellite from the seemingly safer northwest corner of our country, it is quite another to stand here with a bird's-eye view of cataclysm. Consider how charming Seattle would seem, with its bungalows and trees and a multitude of polite rules for giving one one's space, contrasted to this island crowd-together where it's possible to enter the subway in the Upper East

21

Side fantasy of wealth and exit, minutes later, in the burned out wreckage of the Bronx.

I think it is safe to say that the Pacific Northwest has unwound me in many ways, buffered me from such devastating landscapes, and in no way was I prepared for the brutality of this cavern, for what people could do to people, callow as this may sound.

I suppose what I feel is shock, how it makes its way in unmercifully. Because I'm so stupefied by what has been wrought here that I manage it only by closing my eyes and reopening them between taking the longest gasps I've ever breathed in. This is when September Eleventh becomes entirely real for me.

And when I finally rest my eyes, I realize how many men are down there working, which is a far cry from assessing. And how many others are here, too, with emotions that are just now passing from astonishment to weariness, lips quivering as we stare.

I should explain that I'm not proud of how I flirt with a security guard—this tall, jovial man with the accent and attitude of a person born to the boroughs, this man who wears a gold cross studded with diamonds around his clean-shaven neck, this man who looks like an uncle or cousin of mine with a tinsel of gray in Italian-black hair so that I can look easily into the mirror of him—in order to get him to *tawk*. I know flirtation has no place in the presence of such ruin. But in a lifetime, mine anyway, one is seldom privy to such a firsthand account of something so significant, and I can't resist trying to gain something intimate of it for myself. Cheeky, I know, but it worked.

This is when things get really uncomfortable. For a married woman, anyway.

After ten icy minutes of guilty confession (mine) and admonishment (his), he softens and tells me that, *yeah lady*, all of the debris is trucked to Staten Island and placed on top of the largest landfill in the world. That his nephew helps sift through the rubble. And that his accent is Bronx not Brooklyn as I guessed, and then he puts me in my place by saying *lady, you're da one wit da akcent.*

Yet what I find on Church Street, in some ways, is more terrible than the wreckage behind me. An entire block of grief-commerce flourishes. Overnight, this part of town acquired a new economy where anyone can buy a T-shirt branded TERROR! Or a photo of the burning towers complete with a fireman's forged autograph. And when one of the hawkers says to me, *honey, honey, honey, get your souvenir,* it's for this reason I finally cry. Even so, I stay in the area, taking in everything.

Frankly, I don't have the will to write on. Neither do I have the know-how. No clue how to immortalize or to make a tribute out of this essay. Nor can I imagine what will become of a site, or how our nation will choose to commemorate a void that, to my eyes, seems fully whole as is.

AN OLYMPIC-SIZED APOLOGY

February 2002

My mother adores the winter Olympics. Specifically, figure skating. And it's for this reason I decide to watch the games, full of hopes that she and I will be able to converse about something other than family gossip and the sanctity of her arthritis.

I don't like to witness competitive sport. I suppose this began early on when my mother and aunts would compare my siblings, cousins, and me aloud, so that I can hardly stomach seeing such young, pliant athletes compete under the critical eye of the entire world. Each time a skater topples out of a triple axle (that's what they're called, right?), a black cloud passes through me. It's one thing to watch the ready, set, go-for-it of skating, quite another to feel it, receptivity seeping out every pore.

And yet, a week later, I'm fully immersed, unwilling to let go of the drama. I suppose, like most, I welcome an opportunity to see the world come together on peaceful terms. Even if they have gathered by the great Salt Lake to vie for medals, there is no violence involved other than the gouge to my nervous system.

Actually "immersed" might be too formal a word for the way the games now rule my days and evenings so that I float above

24

the rest of my life, gazing down at my comings and goings with a hazy lack of interest. More like I'm hypnotized. I don't miss a single event, even though I'm bored through most of it. Hockey doesn't captivate me, good God who cares. Bobsledding? I ask you, is winning by a 600th of a second really winning? And no matter what feat is described, unless someone somersaults down the hill, every ski run looks pretty much the same to me. Still, the games are in me.

So much for good intentions. My entry into the sports arena, which was to be a bridge for my mother and me, totally backfires. Currently she is not speaking to me. The culprit: allegations of judge tampering. My mother and I disagree, Italian style, about the Canadian skaters. "I'm on board with the French judge!" I yell into the receiver, trying to convince her no one should wear a grey T-shirt while participating in the pageantry of international skating, especially one involving non-technical presentation marks.

But my mother is in love with the Canadian sweethearts-on-ice, Jamie and David, and there is no arguing with her affections. I remind her how Europeans (which most of the judges are, which *she* is) seldom if ever wear athletic wear to an event, as Americans and Canadians do. "Mom, being an athlete doesn't preclude being aware of cultural biases." My mother doesn't appreciate my pulling conversational rank. She hangs up the phone. This is pretty much how it goes with us; one argument negates months of amicability and nothing much ever changes.

The games burn on. And when Michelle Kwan is just about to skate her long program, the phone rings. It's a dear friend calling to confide details of her pending divorce. "I have to call you back," is all I manage to say. I know she is hurt. But, like the true addict I now am, knowing is not will enough to control my actions. I hang up and watch the skating. I can't think about what I have just done to my friend. Sweet Jesus, what has happened to me?

A week later my mother and I are still at it. "Did you watch the closing ceremonies, Mom? The Italians are hosting the next winter games and they staged a fashion show in the middle of their performance. A fashion show! Proving to the world how important costuming is!" Dog with a bone I am. She hangs up again, but this time only after she calls me *stupido*.

I suppose I deserved that.

Our argument reminds me of my first Christmas in Seattle. Newly arrived from the East Coast, I naturally donned my finest. But when I arrived at my new friend's apartment, I was startled by her informality (jeans, bare feet), and the rest of the day seemed off-key as the carols we sang, unceremonious as the T-shirts she and the other guests wore to the table.

The upshot of this story is that I am more educated about the world of short-track and curling. The downside is that the Olympic Games passed like a bright meteor over my life. Then, quickly as they came, they are gone and a silence falls over my evenings. And it looks as though I have some serious apologizing to do to fill in the void.

And not a 100th of a millisecond too soon.

I DID NOT INVEST IN MICROSOFT

March 2002

It's not hard to believe that a town as geographically unique as Port Townsend, Washington, set against a backdrop of mountains and sea and preserved as a Victorian seaport, will draw hordes of people. And hordes more until its downtown becomes the familiar gift-shop scenario, hardware and grocery stores forced to the outskirts, parking lots sprawling them wide as the excess inside.

My favorite anecdote of Port Townsend's transition from interesting place to place of interest is the tear-down of the Thomas Oil cottages at the far end of Water Street to make way for a maritime center whose plan is, and this is the part that kills me, to preserve *history*. Whatever the nature of a "center," it's hardly more interesting than the real thing, is it? And it is why seaports often feel like a theme park rather than a working harbor; it never occurring to city councils that they might have done something differently. Perhaps it's a lot like celebrity: Good to have admirers at first, until we realize our downtown, appeased for tourists, no longer serves us.

And I'm still unsure why F Street, an ample two-lane road weaving through town, was revamped into a suburban thoroughfare, sculptures along it badly chosen by commission, creations so innocuous they connect us to nothing within. I regret this commissioning of art because it doesn't inspire the public. I think trees, elementary as that sounds, would have served us better. All this attention to art-by-committee while working artists are priced out of town? Substituting public-spirited projects for a charitable commitment to artists creates more alienation between a city and its artists rather than less.

Still, the most comforting element, the very thing that defines community, is a commitment by residents to serve it; i.e., improve. But here is where everything muddles. The word "improve" means something distinctly different to everyone.

The fact that more and more homes in Port Townsend are bought by people who don't want or need to live in them doesn't have to pose a problem. But if they drop down by chartered plane, purchase an affordable house (or two or three) as their second (or third or fourth) home, all in an afternoon, and call a contractor to tear it down because it's their version of improving the lot, well, that straightforwardly does.

I know what some are you are thinking. That in America we are free to buy whatever we can afford, free to alter it as our dreams see fit. The only counter I will offer (there are many) is how quickly that assertion fades when the ones who espouse it suddenly find their ocean view deflowered. That's when they rush to city hall en masse, "view rights" suddenly a priority on the council docket.

Only last week I was on my knees in my front yard, trying to ease into dandelion ousting without turning the entire day into a full-blown weeding frenzy. "Hello," was all the man said, reeking of aftershave (and not the good kind but the sort that touches a place of nausea in you) and wearing black loafers with tassels—two clear indications he was not a local but the kind of middle-aged guy who claims the world by sitting in an air-conditioned Redmond-slash-Bellevue office. I tried to meet his eyes, but my glance jumped right back down to those ugly shoes.

And because he was not good at reading body language (I kept whacking the earth with a trowel), he eagerly shared his news: He'd just bought, and I quote, "a tear-down" and he planned to build something "awesome" in its place. Awesome as in gigantic. Built to impress rather than welcome; columns fit for governmental monuments and a three-car garage.

I'm not used to strangers divulging intention so freely. But he was not a subtle man. Again he mistook my silence for interest and proceeded to tell me how he'd invested early in Microsoft, his knowledge of investing mainly pointing out the lack of my own. All said with eyes darting past me as if someone better was due to show up.

I have a lot of strong feelings, but not about investment portfolios. The downside of being a writer? Just when I need a quick comeback, I balk, worry each word, self-edit. Still, I managed to give him one of those look-you-so-and-so looks. And when he walked away leaving behind a louder space than he'd filled, for some reason, the playback was to annoy me the rest of the afternoon as I struggled with a few hard questions. For me, it's always a slow wind around into clarity. Especially when the challenge comes from someone I dislike.

By the end of the day everything I wanted to say came rolling into focus. And I sent the letter as soon as an address was found, easy in a rumor mill this size. Not because I expect him to rethink the square footage it takes to nurture one's life in. Separating him from a mega-home mentality would take dynamite. Or that he'd reconsider plowing down a modest home as rooted to our town as the cedars surrounding it. But because I could not *not* send it.

Dear Mr. Microsoft: You are right. I did not make a conventional investment. However, I invest every ounce of me in a cottage-sized home, unpretentious as the flimsy trellis it hides behind. And this may come as a whopping surprise from a woman with leaves in her hair, but I have amassed a portfolio: a thousand shares of a marriage, solid bonds to friendship with liens against those I've lost to AIDS, cancer, a car wreck on Sims Way. Or the worst unraveling, one meaningless skirmish voiding years of trust so a friend and I live on, though separately. Bottom line: I want the holding restored regardless of the reinvestment it will take.

Each sentence came to me rich as the man who will build his mansion on a cliff doomed to slide into the ocean like sand off a plate because, in order to roll out a turf lawn, he'll likely remove the trees that hold his real estate in place.

Coincidence. That's all it was. Or, who knows, maybe divine intervention. But meeting that man is why I finally took stock, why I formed a private contract between a way of life and me, a merger making a million, no, a ga*zillion* times more sense than a yield of stuff.

ONE STEP AT A TIME
May 2002

It happened last year around this time, when spring moves in so moist and leafy it's difficult to imagine a green any greener: My fingers found a lump. I bolted upright. Life turned upside down. The tumble happened fast.

My fear has a systematic order to it: First, panic heats up and scalds my inner thermal. Then, single-mindedness sets in. I can focus only on the familiar. Next, I clean. In a hurry, everything nice and neat. *Neurotically* neat, as if I can control anything. Ultimately, reality stumbles in and gives way to the facts. At which point, the word cancer enters my life in a whole new way, its grasp seizing every fold of my consciousness.

I don't recall a thing I saw on the drive to the radiology clinic. Nor anything I heard. I do recall sitting in the parking lot, paralyzed with fear, knowing I could summon the courage to deal with things. There was just no part of me that *wanted* to.

Finally, repeating the cliche "one step at a time," I swung open the door to the waiting room. Flies probed the windowpane. Their insistence echoed the fear that buzzed through me, bleak as the freeway I drove to get there. My reaction? Pick up a magazine and swat. I *had* to or they'd have sunk me too deep into the hell of medical confinement.

The waiting wore on. I wiped my nose with the back of my sleeve, gnawed my nails. I thought of my friend Jane, who literally wouldn't hurt a fly and I wondered if I'm too heartless. Too what-the-hell-there's-no-such-thing-as-karma. I decided it didn't matter. I wouldn't be more saintlike anytime soon. And that's when the cover of the magazine-as-flyswatter came into focus. COSMO. Utterly perfect breasts! Why was such a magazine anywhere near this room? Somehow it just didn't seem possible.

After that, the most amazing thing about the day, the very thing that was so affirming and grounding about the day, were two words anyone who's been through this would agree sound better than, well, *anything*: benign cyst. Catapulted into life again, there is no relief as the one I instantly felt.

At home, I googled the words "breast cancer" to find that every three minutes a woman is diagnosed with the disease. I went still inside. Then I did the math, or the kind of math I can handle. For one in every intimate group of us a pin-prick sized cell will sneak up from behind like a hit man. And for those of us caught off guard and then, by some miracle, spared, the question becomes: Am I fated to have lone-breast nightmares for the rest of my life?

Fortunately the cyst didn't need to be removed like a mole or ovary to stave off fate. The only thing cut from me was the ability to take even the smallest thing for granted.

That day was one of my darkest. And yet in terms of gratitude, one of the brightest. My guess is that some terrors befall us so that we come to things that really matter. The thanks I feel still grows. Stronger through writing this.

II.

"*Risk everything! Care no more for the opinions of others. Act for yourself. Face the truth. Have some fun.*"

— Katherine Mansfield

THE SOUND OF A WORD

June 2002

This is a story about dessert. Ho hum. In other words, not of any importance, no insight spread across the page, nothing to live by.

The thing I never expected, though, when I was asked to write a food piece, was how much fun I'd have writing it. With so many enormous issues to ponder, writing about a sugary thrill seemed about as decadent as binging on one. And yet it turned out to be the perfect respite. Beneath my fingertips, layers of cake were formed and I began to laugh out loud. I don't mean to suggest I want to become a food writer, only that if I'm asked to write food-specifically again, I'm there.

In one of my notebooks, the kind of handheld tablet writers carry because there is no such thing as a memory you can trust, I wrote down something I heard a chef say years ago at a cooking demonstration at Williams & Sonoma, where I'd wedged my way into the crowd for the free food and wound up staying because the chef was smart, funny, and clearly loved the fact he captivated a throng of smiling women. When he said, "Some foods are delicious lies that make us believe in heaven" before popping a slice of Tirimisu into his mouth, everyone clapped with pleasure. Why I saved such a banality

I have no idea other than in those early days of writing practice, so many phrases poured into those notebooks for fear they *meant* something.

That and the fact I love the sound of the word *Tirimisu*, the way the word rolls off the tongue in the smoothest of syllables. As if flowing from an artist's brush. Or singing.

Tirimisu was created in Siena, Italy, in honor of a Grand Duke. Originally dubbed zuppa del duca, or the "duke's soup," it was introduced to the United States in San Francisco. And if I were writing text, these facts would suffice. But I'm not and they don't.

So I'll reenter this story with originality:

These days I find any small upset can go a long way when composing an essay. Luckily, I have a backlog of worries. Take yesterday. Cloistered in my office, I was unable to focus, disconnected from my mind and work, frown lines deepening. All I could think of was: nails need filing, eyebrows need tweezing, my head fraught with a zillion distractions. I was tapped out, of words, of sync. No zip. I couldn't draw a single thought out of my gut and onto my screen. Angst filled the room.

I turned off my computer and vacated my office to go for a walk. Walks are the swiftest way (swiftest *healthy* way) to get past oneself. Something about the body moving forward, the present too engaging to give into the past. What a relief to enter a big bright world that wasn't mine.

As soon as my feet hit the pavement, I reached into my pocket. Normally I don't want to be another cell-phoney tweedling along, but I had to do what I always do when I have a problem of this magnitude: Ask my husband to solve it.

"Hon," he said. "You need cake. Get some cake." He need say no more. I knew he knew I was thinking what I knew he was thinking: My wife is a cake-a-holic. Despite the fact that it could theoretically be days in a row, weeks even, when I go without cake. And even though he, my Anglo-Saxon mate, calls the pure culinary art of Tirimisu "cake," I find, and this is not easy to admit, his advice pretty much always fits.

And for sentimentality's sake, Tirimisu was the dessert we served at our wedding when I, so young and aglow, knew nothing about anything, except that I was utterly in love and that my wedding dessert had to be Tirimisu instead of traditional tiers of fluffy frosting gloating from the eye of the table.

Perhaps, subconsciously, I knew I'd find my way to Macrina's Bakery like a K-9 nosing its way to cocaine. Tirimisu is my gastronomic destiny. Just thinking of it sends my spirits soaring, significant to note because Tiramisu literally means "pick me up." And if there's one thing I've learned about disappointment, about life, about *me* is that sometimes a moist mixture of cake and cream is all it takes for an Italian girl to come around.

However, the one time I tried to create this delightfully rich dessert, pouring coffee in a shallow bowl, dipping each ladyfinger without making it soggy, arranging them in long layers, dusting with cocoa powder and triple-cream mascarpone. Well ... my best guess at what went wrong is that I did, in fact, need to whisk the eggs until "stiff peaks" formed and gently add them to the sugar before adding both *gradually* to the cream. Rather than letting the eggs slide en masse from their shells directly into an uncombined heap of ingredients casserole-style. When will I learn it's never wise to rush a delicate thing?

But there are things bakers are expert at, such as perfecting Tirimisu, and things I'm best at, such as wolfing down Tirimisu. It's my true north.

And though writers are trained to root out cliches, is there really a better, insufferably hip way to say *delectable*? Wow, ... I think, as this last line pops out. "What a recipe-of-an-ending."

Precisely. And good to come back to something simple.

GARDENS SAY A LOT
July 2002

Suppose for a minute you wrote a book titled *Women in the Garden*, and you are invited to sign copies at a garden show.

Since that initial invitation, I've learned that garden shows are numerous as the charities they support. So for two summers now I've packed up my books, covering freeways from Seattle to Spokane, turning down a few because I could see myself taking on more of these than I'm wired to handle. For it isn't the gardens that most intrigue, but the social climate entwining each, varied as the plant life.

Completely naive about garden shows, I thought the gardens on display would be similar to our P-patch in Belltown, where a vibrant, unpretentious garden is tucked between Elliott Avenue and Vine Street, gardeners eager to share enthusiasm with nosey onlookers like me.

Then I found myself on the East Side of our city. In Medina. Trust me, had I not been invited as an author, I'm pretty sure my life would not have intersected *this* life.

Those of you not familiar with Medina need to know that Bill Gates lives an estate away from the sheared-for-golf lawn I propped my book table on. When I drove up, foremost on the owner's mind was that my car was not fitting enough to be parked near her tiled piazza. She was obviously suffering from some kind of garden show performance anxiety.

I proceeded to unload my boxes of books before driving off to hide my battered 1989 Dodge Colt, the walk back seeming twice as long now that I felt poor. And the garden? A portal into another universe, as far from where one might say, "Honey, come and look at the size of my delphiniums!" and deep into the world of "Behold what an architect can contrive." To me, enormous landscaped gardens showcasing indigenous foliage are tidy but ungratifying. If I'm promised a show, I expect flora that blooms with colors that reach into me.

Maybe it's my proletariat roots reaching deeper than appreciation can go, but I find myself wondering if the owners of these grounds gaze over their land with pride but from a distance? Unable to grasp a hands-on, I-grew-this-from-seed kind of knowledge? And do these estates need to be so large in order to house the size of the void such a lack of involvement can create?

The next weekend, and what a relief it was, I sunned myself behind a modest bungalow in Wallingford where the owner didn't rope off her aromatic ground cover but invited people to step on it just so we could know the swiftness with which a scent can begin and end. The interconnection of gardener to garden? Fertile as her compost bin in clear sight and steaming.

Today I lounge away the warmest hours in my friend's rooftop garden, where a few hollyhocks sway against the walls of our vertical world. Condo living isn't exactly the greatest seed bed for gardening, and moisture can't seep all that deep up here, but there is some innovation and a few creative rows of bug-eaten lettuce. And it seems to gratify the gardener who enthusiastically calls her container patch "Sofia."

And in my eyes, nothing is more satisfying than pride with a name like that.

FAMILY REUNION
July 2002

I can only write about my family reunion in hindsight. Maybe because there isn't another uniting quite equal to it. I look back and the reasons for going seem obvious, but initially I resisted, staring at my invitation for a while, then hiding it from view.

But as the world shifts beneath my feet, a catastrophe of polit-ical will which is never a good mix when men and might are involved, the personal effect is even larger: An almost feral-like need to connect with those I love.

The Reunion: Upon arriving, I am stunned to see my past in my family's eyes. From then on I'm transfixed every step of the way. Writer-cum-eavesdropper that I am, I immediately scrib-ble a few notes on my cocktail napkin. But instead of feeling like a writer, I feel like a spy. Not the sister, daughter, cousin, niece, and aunt I need to be between breath-catching silences. Because I am so happy to be with people who look like and act like me that I almost burst into tears. The affini-ty I feel is something that will stay with me always.

I must confess here that it's been years, ahem, *twenty* years since I returned to the fold of my family. Living in Seattle can do this to an East Coast transplant trying hard to re-root. I still have a clear mental picture of me, all those years ago, tie-dyed and hitchhiking across the country, leaving home not a decision I needed to think over. Since early on, I knew I had to do the work of finding myself, which meant forging away from family and convention. Only by letting go of the reins could I begin to realize who I was by shedding, mile by mile, who I was *not*.

Yet there is no denying the faces filling the reunion suite belong to the proud people who were there for me before life settled in on us and our roads forked. And with each stride I take across the carpeted lobby, my world stops, like a good listener, to let me move into my family's sphere without hesitation, embarrassment, or any of the feckless emotions that define the wandering, restless will of an immigrant's daughter.

Which brings me back to why, sitting around a table in a Manhattan supper club where photos of Frank Sinatra and Joe DiMaggio hang in gilded frames over the bar, I am reminded just how far I've strayed. Because, even though I wear my best silk dress from the Banana Republic, to the women of my family, unless your clothing has shoulder pads and sequins you are *not* dressed up. And when Cousin Johnny actually says "badda-bing, badda-boom" for emphasis, I laugh out loud. Worse, when he stands by the door with his chin up and arms crossed behind him looking like a bouncer hired for our reunion, I joke that I feel like I'm on the set of "The Sopranos." This is where he shoots me a look with those thick black eyebrows of his to let me know we are simpatico but I'd better put a lid on it. Then he hugs until he lifts me right out of my too-big-for-me heels. From that point on, we are cousins again. But only after I nod to a second round of antipasto am I fully trusted again. Because he is not, I soon discover, any-where near amenable enough to consider the word "vegetarian."

I don't let this bother me. To my family, food is tantamount to religion, and you don't stray from its consecrated dictum. This might be my life, but it is their Holy Eucharist.

But don't a lot of my friends in Seattle define a huge part of themselves by what they will or will not eat? And isn't there usually some form of food politics to contend with in the com-pany of any group of Americans who feel entitled to their likes and dislikes no matter what? Case in point: Recently I attended a potluck gathering, the kind Wallingford is known for, where I felt enough peer pressure to stop myself short of saying that after, say, three months of not eating a slice of meat comes a day when I just have to have a blood-oozing rib-eye. And in that particular moment, anything resembling tofu, frankly, won't come close to cutting it.

There was a time I thought there was no better honesty than to assert my take on the world no matter what company I was in. But I've learned that some things, especially while in a politically appropriate neighborhood where women still dress as if it were the '60s, are better left unsaid. However, when the no-dairy vegan-vegetarian spoke out in support of the Native American's right to slaughter another innocent whale, I had to challenge her convictions no matter how many times my husband kicked me under the table.

Mentally, I compare this to my family's food issues at hand: Whether a pound of pasta per person is enough to serve. How, as soon as lunch is over, conversation shifts to supper.

In most instances, I don't try to give my family a view of my life they can identify with. Or of my city, a city that can feel, especially during local elections, as segregated as the deep South. Not by race, but ideology. Or how its people eagerly espouse cultures other than their own as if searching for an identity (think Tibetan prayer flags snapping over Scotch-Irish foyers) and how this differs from my family's way of embracing only their own culture. For how does one begin to describe a city with less of an ethnic culture and more of an all-encompassing, cautious nature, a city that encourages a near desensitizing sensitivity, to people who have never viewed conversation as a tool to think hypothetically? And yes, I'm aware of my family's provincialism, but when you get right down to it is there any real difference between meditation crystals and rosary beads if peace of mind is all you're after?

When I first went away to college, I remember hanging a sign on my door that read YOU ARE NOT YOUR FAMILY! Ah, but everything I've discovered since then is that I am, in ways I can choose to carry forward, ways I can work to let go of, and in ways I cannot adjust the alignment of no matter how diligently I try.

To my great surprise, and as exhausted as it made me, I climbed back up the rungs of our family tree. And what did I learn? That I now have a fighting chance to make whole my life and work. That I can turn a new leaf into, say, a new tree. And finally, that family, however you define it, asks us to reach a little higher, do something more, make the extra effort.

CONTENTMENT

August 2002

There was a time when I didn't know an annual from a perennial; when, if I were asked by another to pick a sprig of rosemary, I could not tell it from a twig of lavender, nor did I care. Gardening was for older women who needed to retreat from life, right? I remember informing the realtor who sold us our home that, from the look of things, the garden surrounding the property would have to fend for itself. I had a lot of goals to tackle back then, gardening was not one of them.

It was about a year later when, after hours of writing in my office, I stood to stretch. And what I saw on the other side of the fence was my elderly neighbor watering a withered garden gone to seed weeks ago. Still, the grounded-ness of her effort was hard to miss. Spraying water from an uncoiled hose lent serenity to her whole, smooth face, her white hair a stark contrast to the brightness in her eyes. I was envious. Not as in coping with jealously, but envy in its purest form: a curious, intense feeling that awakens you, cell by cell, conveying just what needs to change about your life if, like me, certainty is what you are ultimately after.

For the longest time I stood there watching how the effort made her to lean into the flow as if she longed to follow each silver droplet spilling its way down. And I could see how

45

watering is what's left to a gardener too frail to weed or dig. Spellbound, I watched as if through an aperture, seeing clear through to the quieting-down life becomes.

Writing can be isolating. No one on the periphery cheering you on. I welcome ways to balance this solitude, ways to turn my writing routine on its side and be in the company of others. And so, after weeks of, well, spying on my neighbor, I walked through the gate and into her yard to introduce myself.

In a word, contentment. That's what I felt from her, a combination of acceptance and satisfaction I long to possess but haven't exactly pinned down. I realized that I needed something to ease an inner absence that was growing. The next day, completely and inevitably, her discipline became mine.

Since then, my yard has transformed. I learned that a garden, like life, doesn't reward those too eager, impatient, or greedy. Next, I noticed how digging into soil was affecting my work in unexpected ways: Fear seemed to ease off, to compost on its own. And I began to see others differently, as if each of us stands in a garden of our own, so to speak, tilling a private corner of the world. My garden, basic in its earthly needs, was yielding more and more of an ethereal return.

Now when writing feels too aloof, or when insecurities surge to the surface, I escape to my maze of color until all of me is returned to me.

And as my neighbor holds to her task of watering, I hold to mine. In our gardens, we thrive in a total absence of pretense. Which helps explain the deceptive simplicity of gardening: a deeply gratifying thing, whatever it is, that binds us to ourselves, to others, to earth.

A FEW THOUGHTS ON THIS
March 2003

In the last months, all I cared to believe is that our president had sunk his teeth into Iraq and refused to let go. That wrath and revenge had spread inside his pumped-up chest. That he was itching for a war in order to satisfy some inner rage. Mostly, I wondered if my dislike of him made me want to discount him. I admit, I'm often capable of this.

Then I listened to his televised address and to hours and hours of congressional debate on whether to pass a resolution that would grant, without restriction, the certainty of war, and I realized, with utter embarrassment, how much I'd missed in all this.

Now, I'm terrified. Not only of biological and chemical weapons, but because I don't know whom to trust. Are those who support the invasion of Iraq warning us about a madman, information anyone of conscience would run with? Or, like good defense lawyers, are they less about truth and more concerned with what we, the jury of voters, will hear? Because no one mentions that no other country has used more weapons of mass destruction than the United States. Even I wasn't prepared for this fact. But the fact emerged regardless.

In the wake of September 11, I consciously tried to get back on track, to not let a little thing like the world gone mad stop me from reentering my good life, mankind no match for my tenacious will. Now, I cram to catch up, naivete sliding away. And this new awareness, this surrender of hope, well, I begrudge it completely. Which is why when Madeline Albright bravely spoke out against the war, I trembled with gratitude from a place inside me no man in politics has ever reached.

In the same breath, I fear Hussein if he does, in fact, garner weapons. Which is likely. Because, and at what point do we make this the question, didn't I read that our country sold them to him at a point in time behind us?

At this writing I sense there is much more to the neurotic situation between Hussein and Bush than we are being told, and that what we are being told is fabricated, what our leaders concoct behind closed doors in order to make their lies real. What Lyndon Johnson did when he told congress that U.S. ships were fired upon by North Vietnamese in the Gulf of Tonkin when the firing never happened. The same when Reagan invaded Grenada after telling Congress that Americans on the island were in danger. Turns out the only danger they were in was the likelihood of being hit by U.S. fire.

I read these accounts of the past, crystal-clear in the way they blur everything our president says.

I react to politics on a visceral level. My gut tells me war is wrong so war is wrong. Maybe that's why none of the rhetoric taking shape on either side of the issue seems to belong to me, why I can't remember a word of it. Because, by nature, writers cling to somewhere not of a defined political or religious position, but to an individuality within. Precisely why regimes kill us off first.

Even as I say this, I can feel myself erupting from it's own need to make a change. One I don't want to make: from optimist to realist, if for no other reason, so that I can acknowledge that the world will never be anything but at odds with itself, that some huge primitive instinct within men to revert to warfare allows them to justify our soldiers as sacrificial lambs.

Yet, just when I think I can accept this, the whole pragmatist thing, I imagine a world where peacemakers hold us together with intellect and negotiation (imagine!) because that's what we've entrusted them to do, what leadership is *supposed* to do, and it's the only thought that brings any satisfaction to me whatsoever.

But it doesn't so much matter what my imagination can suppose, does it? Justness still takes a back seat to the fact that we continue to empower men who wage war as a means to an end, as if it's their world and not ours, as if they came into this world by their own manly means and can do with the planet what they like.

I'm guessing you know the end to this essay, with the headlines being what they are and, I'm afraid, will be again. Would someone please explain to me how these same militarists can question how our teenagers can pick up a rifle and blow away their schoolmates? Have they forgotten or, more likely, never realized the essence of children, how perceptive they really are?

A WRITER'S DILEMMA
April 2003

For months now, no matter what I start to write about, Iraq intervenes. "So write about that," my husband says, "the dilemma for writers in war time."

Honestly, in our marriage how many times can he be so right?

With the unrelenting urgency of invasion behind us, as far as the news business goes, I watch and read how the media fumbles to balance life for an audience tiring of military reality, swiveling to whatever story will hold it.

As a writer, I seek my own sense of balance. And in this overwhelmingly masculine state of world affairs, as a woman. Daily, I weigh my instincts against government's, finesse against militance, moving between disbelief and anger. The tentacles of this war have invaded every wavelet of emotion within and it all comes down to this: Our country embarrasses me. And no part of me will get through this shame unaffected.

And shame keeps me from equalizing. Dishes are stacked in the sink, bills go unpaid. Yet, here I sit researching the history of G.I. Joe dolls (oh, wait, *action* figures), and everything I find attests to gender dissimilarity right from the get go. No "girl toy" manifests war as such blatant, hands-on fun. And that's nothing compared to the war-in-action video games that drive home the message of killing-as-problem-solver. So, in man's defense: Do you think we still prime our baby boys for war from some kind of ancient instinct to ensue our very survival, no matter how horrendous battling methods have become?

As for my reaction to this question, yesterday in a convenience store I spotted a collection of model Stealth bombers and felt the urge to crush them into bits. Instead, I dropped several of them from sight, reminding myself that I can't adjust the world, though that's exactly what I *was* doing by concealing the planes behind a bin of Nerf Balls.

And I carried out this hiding-of-the-war-toys, with the debate of an E.B.White poem playing in my mind: I arise in the morning/ torn between a desire to improve the world/ and a desire to enjoy the world. I memorized the poem in my first year of college, back when my political awareness was defiant, yes, but unwilling to stretch beyond idealism. How I'd love to reconnect to that girl again, to experience anew such naivete, to burst into my day without this concentration on worldly trouble, to see our flag waving and not feel guilt like a weight hanging from my neck.

Because, know what, I'm tired of guilt, of putting too much pressure on myself to understand the understandable. My goal is to balance again, or my household will crumble along with the last statue of Saddam. Besides, it's not the details of this war I care about anymore. Only possibility matters, that this war might bring about a shift in consciousness, finally, and that the masses will, at last, view war as futile. That's all I look for between the lines.

One last thing: What keeps me most off-kilter is voice; everyone's so loud that I have trouble hearing my own. Take the woman who drove me home from a reading I gave last week. When I confided my uncertainty about every issue concerning warfare, she responded by banging her hands on the steering wheel, shouting that there is no ambiguity about war! Essentially silencing me with willfulness—the very act she denounced about our government. I sat there thinking how only those steeped in denial can dismiss that this world is full of ambiguity. It's gotten to where I'm saddened if the subject of war doesn't come up, and dread when it does.

But the loudest voice belongs to a young woman I sat next to on a bus yesterday. Because of her dreadlocks, I assumed her political sympathies would mirror my own. They didn't. She was reading a newspaper story about the war. So I made a seditious comment about how am I to believe anyone can make a democracy out of a culture that still beheads people. That's when she looked me square in the eyes and said, "My little brother is, like, fighting over there so shut the fuck up."

Red-faced with humility, a change came over me and I don't know what trued up inside, exactly, but I was ready to tie yellow ribbons around my cedar trees and raise a flag from my antenna if that's what the girl needed to get through this. Shame-saturated, I tried to picture myself in her shoes, and that's when it dawned on me that to the families who send their children off to serve and die, supporting them doesn't mean I support war. Of course, to the many who will see any such "dawning" as something akin to treason, it does.

So I will remind them that democracy's most basic element is freedom of thought and speech. Exactly what our president says we've gone to Iraq to establish while here at home we struggle with the concept and rage at one another.

Because of a chance encounter on a bus, my new faith has become this: If a woman suffers because her brother, husband, or son might come home prone in a plastic sack, I support her and politics be damned.

That's enough certainty, anyway, to keep me sane through all this.

SOME SONGS SHAPE
US FOR LIFE
March 2003

Perhaps the most crucial aspect of a choreographer's work is remembering.

Music has the uncanny ability to throw us into longings and letdowns we've pushed aside in real life. Recently, as I listened to the Ricki Lee Jones song "Don't Let the Sun Catch You Crying," pow, all at once, the memory of falling into desperate teenage love sat itself plunk down in the pit of my stomach, the ache of being dumped by my first real love.

I bought the song. Then, alone in my studio, I moved to it. Carefully at first. Then with abandon. A process that can, with any luck, lead me toward the dance I want to create as a subtle shift takes place within. Over the years, I've noticed one of these shifts is often forgiveness.

But no one lets go of deeply held hurts in one session of creativeness. One has to be ready. I must have been willing, finally, to forgive that boy for kisses that burned through my lips and cremated my common sense. And for ignoring me soon after.

Ever since September Eleventh, the song I hear over and over in my head is, "War! Uuhh! What is it good for? Absolutely nothin'!"—that gritty tune of social commentary I sang at the top of my lungs during the Vietnam War. Some songs shape us for life.

My reaction was to go to work creating a horrifying piece. Boots marching. Bodies lying still as mannequins. What I mean is, real.

But I couldn't finish. I took the first step only to find I *couldn't* take a second. The reason for my inability? I can't seem to find a thread to tie this segment of history together. Uncertain how to pinpoint an opening, a middle, a finale, it's unclear whom I need to forgive; our bullying leaders or all of mankind? Of what to express about the horrific problem and underlying issues of war, a problem so vast and complicated that it could never be explained to me in a way that would make any sense. And by "make sense" I don't mean militant or political reasons for war, rationalizations too immoral to consider, unless I want to compose a dance that reveals a dark and crouching presence emanating from behind a scrim of even darker proportions.

And with no acceptable explanation, how can I interpret such meaninglessness through the limbs of my body? It would no longer be a dance but a march of protest, the choreography confused and stormy, like dancing in anger at your parents while you're still a teenager. And there is only one official rule for the making of choreography: Know What You Are Trying To Express.

I abandoned the piece. Not because I couldn't meet the challenge, but for two other reasons. One is that I decided not to leave my audience with war on its shoulders. Instead, I circled back to the parts of life that strengthen and renew, where we need to rest in order to cope.

Secondly, if I don't have some fun with my choreography my battery dies.

So, to honor the life of Barry White, I composed a medley of his songs as our finale. *My darling I can't get enough of your love, babe.*

Because war is what it is: Artless. Madness. And not one of us can transform it, certainly not I, through dance or otherwise, into something aesthetic.

THE BOOK SIGNING
April 2003

A week ago I gave a reading at a bookshop in a suburb of Seattle. The event, held to honor National Poetry Month, was a literary staging of my latest book, *The Immigrant's Table*, a combination of poems mixed with heirloom recipes handed down from the women in my family. To segue into each poem, I tell stories about my "moonstruck" family in the most Italian of settings: around a dinner table.

After the reading, I was signing copies when a man rushed over to say, "Your stories are wonderful! You should write a book!" His words sent my stomach to the floor. And the thing that got me most was the expression on his face. He was dead serious. I wondered what he thought I'd just read *from* at my *book* reading held in a *book*store?

When you live downtown in Seattle as I do, within walking distance of independently owned, poetry-supporting bookstores such as Elliott Bay Books and Queen Anne Books, a bus ride away from Open Books, a bookstore that sells poetry exclusively, and poetry readings are popping up in even the most unlikely cafes, it's easy to believe poetry lives in the hearts and minds of many Americans. But I'm reminded whenever I step back into the mainstream that poetry is a bit more, what is the word, imperceptible.

Take my father. Though he didn't come to this country until the age of twenty-five and faced a multitude of prejudices thereafter, he is now the quintessential, golf-obsessed, Costco-shopping American man. In fact, during our last phone call he said I was "unpatriotic" subsequent to my saying that if an army invades the victims of a tyrant, it's sort of like saying, "Hey listen, why don't we kill you and then you can get on with your life." And when I reminded him that freedom of expression *is* the cornerstone of a democracy, his lash-out was to call me "un-American." Whatever.

The analogy I'm trying to make is that arguing about the hypocrisy of our government with my father could turn out as arduous as explaining to the man who urged me to write a book why I write poetry. But that won't stop me from trying.

I'm not poking fun here, well, maybe a little. The point is: Though my father has the decency to display my books of poetry on his coffee table, he still asks me, "When you gonna write a real book, huh?" Meaning novel, mystery thriller, or self-help manual of the week, and speaking for many like him who rarely look beyond bestsellers sold at grocery chains. I've managed to refrain from asking him if he's actually *read* one of my books, wanting to preserve our little feat of keeping our debates worldly in nature rather than personal.

This month, in honor of National Poetry Month and my father (also my mother because how else am I going to show her this?), I offer a poem because it's poetry I write when the purest form of happiness comes over me: gratitude for a life

I'm fortunate enough to lead. Or when the weight of pain is
so dense I can't reach past it any other way:

NORTHWEST TOMATOES

My hands are my mother's hands,
the same fan-shaped nails and transparent skin
revealing a crosshatch of blue.

Yet, my father's need to dig into soil
to make salads grow is what I renew
each short, warm season
when my single row of blight ridden tomatoes
results in a harvest I hold in one hand.

I've taken to wearing yellow-lens sunglasses
(my friend swears they ward off the blues)
to imagine each green fruit bolting
fully ripe and sweet, shade so deep
it nears black where stems rise from the pulp
ample enough to puree into all
my girlhood is held in:
My father's tomato garden,
my mother's sauce
that smudges my chin and stains
my life red.

RESOLUTION
May 2003

This evening, I'm one in the horde of commuters on the Bainbridge Island ferry, the megawatts of downtown swaying behind us as we cross the sound. I'm a once, maybe twice-a-weeker, but for the mass of men and women besieging this ship, the scenic ride is simply an everyday passage from here to there.

But on a night like this, when stars come out by the zillions and the Columbia Tower rears over the city like a mother over her brood, more riders come topside, making their way up the stairwell to be relieved of work for a while, at least of its potency, worries carried out to sea, lives remembered.

Mid-sound, a silhouette of Mount Baker arises, the great crest that straddles a fault restless as the two boys who run by me. After one tumbles, then just as quickly reassembles his pride with every muscle posed against humiliation, he laughs uncontrollably, "ha ha, ho ho, hee hee," and I swear he is the most lighthearted I've seen anyone, ever.

"Ah," I say, as it hits me: I need more uncensored releases of pure laughter. More joy all around.

Breakthroughs are such small, full-size things. No matter how we make our way into them.

Lovely want, but I'm not one for making resolutions. Even when a part of me, tries hard to wind around a good intention, I can end up failing. Still, I vow right here on this steel ship to definitely, absolutely, laugh more often. Even when I find myself in the company of those who, for whatever reason, haven't given themselves permission to find much humor in life. Maybe it's all the rain, I don't know.

When I'm not in Seattle, or ferrying to and from Seattle, I live in a small town that lies at the end of a road at the end of a peninsula where many have settled as far from biological pasts as geographically possible. Here, men and women practice self-analysis in lieu of religions cast off. And new age-isms reel around in order to fill as many inner vacuums. Add to the mix, long, dark, wet winters and it can feel drably serious at times, virtue as a way of life seeming, well, flat.

Frankly, I long for a bit of hell-raising now and again, a good dose of my Uncle Pete, an irreverent, life of the party, chain-smoking, Cadillac driving, scotch drinking, salt of the earth man everyone loves. Even his eyes grin. And much like the boys who race by me again, laughing and plopping into a seat wearing absurdly baggy pants appropriately low-waisted but alarming all the same.

As our ferry pulls up to the island. I watch a few tourists turn toward the relief map on the wall. I grin at their huddled enthusiasm, envy their eagerness, the surge of fascination we feel when a place is new.

In the space of a single commute and against the risk of twice failing, I make a second pact: to see the beauty of this green and peopled land with the eyes of a newcomer. As if I carry a backpack and wide-angle lens. As if, when the ferry nudges the dock, I feel the wobbling for the very first time.

SOLID BALLAST
June 2003

This year, I decide, dad deserves to be honored on Father's Day with more than retail tradition i.e., a new shirt or canister of golf balls.

Straight away, my decision prompts me to tap out a few lines regarding the complexness of our father-daughter relationship, trying to get to the truth of us while my thoughts are running hot.

Just as passionately, I tear up the page. The will to be honest drops from me. This kind of purge might be natural to a writer, but I'm quite sure it would sink its teeth into my dad. And possibly, hopefully, I'm outgrowing the need to figure out so much.

So I reach back for another memory, and I find this one of Bella.

When I was maybe six, my father traveled to Naples, Italy, his homeland, for what seemed to a kid a very long time. Not knowing whether to fear his absence or enjoy the solace it seemed to bring to our otherwise female household, it did occur to me to ask my mother why he'd left, though I never did. Maybe it was the belittling way my aunt *tsk-tsked* his going in the first place that stopped me, I don't know, but her sigh before saying that it must be nice to have money to throw around left me with that image for days, of my father somewhere far away tossing dollar bills into the air. A child's comprehension is so literal.

When he returned, he surprised me with a life-size porcelain doll, Bella, a doll I named after the word my father called her, twice, as he set her on my bed for the first time. *Bella. Bella.* A doll with starched crinolines flowing over my bed in tiers of Holly Communion or wedding day white lace.

To me, the wary way my father handled her demonstrated what he thought of little girls, little girls meaning *me*, in general: fragile as china. Like one of my grandmother's Hummels, the doll was a statuette to be gazed at from afar but not fooled with. And every time I looked at her, I saw what I was not.

I've never given thought to the other gifts he returned with: a sterling horn-shaped charm I still wear, or the tiny cream-colored boxes of honey and hazelnut *Torrone* for my sisters and me to share. I consider only Bella, pinpointing her as the turning point to my assuming the role as a girl who mowed the lawn instead of helped with housework. At such a tender age, I was already trying to circumvent the psychological distance between the sexes, no part of me wanting to identify with the seemingly less exciting, traditional image of my stay-at-home mom, that if I were more boy-like, the differences between my father and me would lessen. That if I let femininity trickle in, it might wash me right out of his life.

My father led a life typical for men of his generation, fathering babies because it was the appropriate thing to do after marriage. And while my siblings and I grew up secure in knowing he'd work hard and never leave us to fend for ourselves, we also accepted that due to his work and 1950s mindset about all responsibilities concerning childcare (meaning they were my mother's), he wasn't going to be around all that much, either.

My dad's fathering was never, *ever*, as hands-on as the men today I see with Snuggli'ed newborns pressed against their paternal chests. Still, I've come around to knowing he was solid ballast in those early years, as he is still in this wobbly ship of me.

And even though I can fall off-kilter in his presence, awkward in a way that returns me, in a matter of seconds, to somewhere between a toddler and a blithering teenager, I can't imagine myself in this world without him.

Nearly forty years after I last picked up Bella, I remember how beautiful she was. Every detail of her cleft chin and brown eyes still present as if she were next to me here, too big and baptismal on the bed.

This last paragraph, free of all that came before, are the words I finally sent.

III.

"*Advice is what we ask for when we already know the answer but wish we didn't.*"

— Erica Jong

THE APPRENTICE
June 2003

I'll begin by saying that I would rather live in the Northwest than anywhere else in the world. Okay?

That said, I'll try to put into words how it feels to be of Mediterranean descent, both of genes and mind, while wearing fleece pajamas, heat turned up, cat refusing to go outside. In *summer*.

My neighbor describes our Northwest June as a band warming up. A band that won't play until July, takes a break mid-August, and leaves the stage for good in September. "And if it's an El Niño year," she says emphatically, "temperatures are warmer in February than we can expect from May." And when she adds we're due for one wet fall, an urge to weep sweeps over me, making even the smallest appreciation of gray skies, or her for that matter, utterly impossible.

I'm sure you're wondering why I stay in a place with such a short summer, the same question I've asked myself for the last twenty years soon as August fades. Is it the richness that follows the rain, so immensely beautiful I can hardly believe my eyes? Or have I integrated with the words gurus and therapists like to recite: that whatever annoys us most is the one thing we most require?

Because the answer is clear: Nothing keeps me writing like sky dark as my eyes and hair. The moist smell of grass renewing its roots is a tendon that ties me to my work, that takes me seriously apart as I dig in toward the center of my life a word at a time. Whereas if sun shines, I'm likely to be miles from home, immersed in the holiest of holy sunlit greens that is everywhere and everything around me.

Still, each fall, say, five minutes into October, my mood dips. Soon after, I make a conscious effort not to bore my friends with weather-whining (still, it's in the air, let me tell you, it's in the air). When the skies refuse to lighten for days on end, the groove between my eyebrows deepens further, the physical effect of gray on my emotions when what I'm feeling gets stuck between my eyes.

And sometimes I'm so far on the other side of glad to hear that more rain is predicted that I'm reminded no matter how many years I live in the Northwest, I'll always be an apprentice, never as rooted as my friend who calls herself a B&R (born and raised), the distance between our weather preferences insurmountably vast.

How we differ, she and I. She views the gray weight of sky as a recipe for cozy. And while she considers the cost of water a necessity for lawn maintenance, watering hers in August until it's a putting green of perfection, my yard is a weedy patch kindling beige. She goes after dandelions as if by gunpoint; I add them to salads. Still, in her company, I hold on to every syllable of Northwest-ness, as if I'm part of her convivial group. If not by understanding at least *looking* as if I understand, because unlike my desire for blue above, she longs for turbulence. And I long for a friend just like her.

And when we walk under a sky fueled with warmth, she stares upward at clouds peeled back, the look in her eyes as if she doesn't remember how soon squalls will saturate the bluffs until they slide like quicksand into the jaw of March sea. Or collapse over the one road leading out of this bed and breakfast town, until those here for a stint of quiet are unsure, suddenly, just *how* quiet they want things to be.

SMALL TOWN
— dedicated to Elmer Stanton

July 2003

Graciousness is always at its most tenuous when two people want utterly different things and neither will budge. This is when we might want to find the compromise, but figuring it out can be tough. Sometimes the best thing, the only thing, to do is give in and live with the results.

There is an integral oneness to the world, and most people experience it in nature. I feel it when I'm writing. My office is the one place that lets me compile the slivers of me and piece them together. It's my temple surrounded by lavender I grew from seed. Sitting here, with a ringside view of the world, makes me happy in such immediate ways.

Yet, temple or no, my mailman admits he's afraid of bees. And lavender pulses with bees, yellow jackets too. But wait. Is this man suggesting I clip the lavender that scrapes my office door with its metal mail-flap that opens only for him?

At first, I refuse to even consider it. Sorry. No can do. But there is no escaping the fact that in the front-yard world of "Mailman versus Mail Receiver," like it or not, the Mailman is boss.

There is a wide range of copacetic ways to relay desire, especially if you're afraid to come right out and ask for what you want. My mailman's style might be manipulative, but it's efficient, efficiency being the whole point of a uniform, right?

Still, I tend to hold to what favors me. To lavender tapping my windowpane, curving its opulent way through space till it falls into place beside me. To purple seeds on my sidewalk like bits of gravel with no weight.

I stand my ground, daring my mailman's dread of bees to change my life in any way.

Yet, Catholic-born, my guilt has a way of gathering like possibility or the downside of possibility: fear. I clip the lavender. Some here. A little there. Until I've pruned its size along with my attitude, pungent branches littering my soft square of lawn, the spiked odor of evergreen briny in my nose.

It will take time to fill in the years, but I figure I'll learn to bend with the limbs I left whole. And, much like me, the shrub will have to find new ways of reaching into the world if it expects to grow.

This is hardly a life-altering story of small town living, but I think life alters enough already. Today an eager mail recipient and a less agitated mailman are a team again, which, when you get right down to it, is crucial to a writer.

AFTER THE FIRE
August 2003

The day before Port Townsend's Aldrich's Market, the oldest continually running grocery store in Washington state, burned down, I was sitting in a café on Polk Street in San Francisco, engaged in a "city versus small-town" conversation with a woman who'd lived in an apartment behind Aldrich's for years before moving to San Francisco. We agreed Aldrich's Market was what we cherished most about our uptown way of life: "uptown" referring to the part of town that lies uphill from the sea, where Victorian ladies once resided away from the grimy docks downtown. The fact we didn't need to drive, suburban style, to purchase our food meant we could walk closer to our ideal of how life should be.

Since tourism is currently Port Townsend's first industry, it's fair to say I ignore many of its shops unless my mother is visiting. My capacity to pay little mind to trinkets is endless. I can summon no energy to care about bath soaps, scented candles, or dollhouse miniatures no matter what city I'm in. My daily trek is simple: a walk downtown to Don's Pharmacy when I need, well, just about anything; the coffee cart outside of Swain's; back uptown to the post office if I have time to stand in line. Last stop before home: Aldrich's Market, my arms in a bear-hug around my sack of groceries.

Aldrich's was like a social or, even better, a social I didn't need to stay long at. I could stand around and join in the gab or be a part of the gathering from the privacy of myself, the intimate size of the store welcoming me either way, perfect for someone like me whose meal of choice is two hard-boiled eggs, a couple of carrots, maybe an apple, and some wine and cheese.

As soon as I entered Aldrich's, the wood floors and piles of produce rearranged the modern world of grocery shopping to my liking. Some shopping experiences are simply more aesthetic, more genuine than others. I can still see the avocado bin in front of me. Lettuce to my left. Coffee near the tortillas. These images, these presences absent, are the food vocabulary of my eyes closed.

And more than once I've set out to buy something, peddling my bicycle nearly there, before remembering the fire. The fire that left me reeling. Then again, I grew up in the era of "Jaws." It seems some great white toothy shark is always swimming beneath me. I'm never as bowled over as I should be.

Now what?

QFC is so "up the hill" it might as well be in Sequim.

Safeway is too macro. I know people feel comforted by so much choice, but I dread it (unless we're talking shoes). And shouldn't there be a third option for transporting the makings of dinner through a store roughly the size of Rhode Island? My choices are either a plastic basket that hangs from my arm like an awkward handbag, or a Costco-sized cart fit for a robust family of five.

This leaves The Food Co-op. But that has always felt too—I search for a word—political for me. To recall a friend's words about working there: "Nothing is more uncooperative than a co-op." Because when I pass through its sliding doors, I do get this whiff of something, something other than food, what dispute might smell like.

Aldrich's was my consummate grocery store, my niche.

Honored that my poem hung on its wall over by the meat cul-de-sac before disappearing with the rest of the store into unrelenting flames, I end with it. Like birds that sing after a storm, I rejoice in what remains:

STANDING IN LINE AT ALDRICH'S GROCERY

On a summer morning,
if sun casts its warmth without hesitation,
we chat up the likeliness of tomatoes
actually ripening, how good it feels
to sleep with windows wide open
while curtains billow the air.

Or else only a nod
relayed through the line
as we cup cups of coffee
sometimes nothing to say.

Or, because we share so much: The same friend
whose marriage climbed, peaked, and severed.
The same children springing into the store at noon.
The same neighbor whose cancer rose

and spread like fluid between her limbs...
we find a reason
to air confusion, joy, amazement, fear—
especially fear
when it sweeps through the pit of our stomachs

briskly as the wind mounting outside
when fall is fully engaged, forcing us to crouch,
run to our cars, climb in
disheveled, angled

before righting ourselves, our bags
this blustery season, its dim light
lingering over those still inside

moving ahead in line and closer
to revealing some new remnant
or candid glimpse
of our entangled lives.

Word on the street is that the rebuild of Aldrich's Market will
be fully operable by the summer of 2005. I like the image of a
community waiting as long as it takes while a renaissance
takes as long as it needs.

TANGO HEARTED
September 2003

I love to social dance, but you can hardly call me adept. I dance because I enjoy it. It gets me out of my office and, more importantly, out of my head till I'm transported to a place hard to name but not to give in to as I fall into step with the world.

This month I'm taking a tango class. Not because the instructor is a gorgeous Argentinian with a muscular build of fine proportion, or that the swarthiness of his hair dissolves into the swarthiness of his eyes, no *no*, but because I bask in any endeavor that requires a new dress.

Somewhere in my consciousness, I've always longed for a clingy, black satin gown with a peekaboo slit clear up my silky thigh, preferring it ten-fold over the cotton frock I bought for swing dance class where I never quite took to hop-skipping around fixed from the waist up. Which just goes to show, sometimes you have to make a mistake just to be free of it.

Oh. My. I'm wearing nylon stockings for the first time since, um, senior prom. Living in Seattle, legs encased in thick, cotton tights, can cause one to forget just how sleek synthetic fibers can *be*. One minute my legs are sandpaper, every hair follicle a scratchy flaw, the next I'm running my hands up and down the smooth surface of me. If satisfaction has a physicality, it is surely this.

The only problem is, despite my desire to look the part, stiletto heels are a bit of a problem. But only if I try to *walk* in them. Which I do, wobbling to the No. 8 bus that whisks me from downtown to Capitol Hill. Upon boarding, all eyes fix on my heels as if they are a danger to myself and others, or some kinky secret is stuck to their soles. Even a confidant woman such as myself can only take so many gym shoe-wearing strangers staring at her feet from the corner of their eyes.

But the most uncomfortable thing, the very worst thing of all, happens during class (the very *first* class), when I fall flat on my behind. Which is all right. Martha Graham said a fall proves a dancer is willing to risk. Still, drowning in a spasm of embarrassment, I laugh and blame my shoes. Easy. No one questions this in Seattle, home to soles flat as the sidewalks they cruise.

We're not trying to win a contest here; there's only me to please, so why do these dips and leans make me so self-conscious? And it doesn't help that my partner has a shell around him, thick as a geoduck's, with no smile of greeting as he pushes another man out of the way in his haste to grab my hips and pull me to him. Right now I want him to release me and choose another partner! And ... I half mean it.

Let me get this straight, does he honestly believe his scrappy commands will help me unwind? Riddled with impatience, I say, "Listen, I'm no tango dancer. I'm tango-hearted, but hardly the real McCoy." He rolls his eyes. God, he makes my hairs sprout gray.

So much for the tender duet I'd hoped for. I found the whole thing scathingly competitive. It seems even on the dance floor, there is always the matter of power. Some nights there isn't enough space, even in the sanctum of The Century Ballroom, for the size of the ego.

I walk home in stocking feet, heels swinging in hand, a faded dancing girl.

I *will* say this: I still want a dance that can move me round the floor with a lighthearted mind. And in that respect, tango class sort of failed me, but not the tango. Because tonight, alone in my boudoir (translation: Murphy bed pulled down from my living room wall), I am *ze most beeyuuteeful tango dancer in ze world.* Just ask my cat.

And when I call a friend to share the details of my evening, blow-by-blow, she tells me about a belly dance class where live Middle Eastern music instantly relieves you from the weight of yourself. Before you know it, she says, you're moving without a care in the world. No partner to maneuver. Amen.

I aim my imagination at the thought of a class like that.

I figure a dancer must seize every opportunity to dance, right? It's not that I'll likely get the hang of how to shimmy my pelvis at hummingbird speed. What propels me to call the instructor is a familiar yen spreading through me, the nerve it will take to try. Because I like a challenge. I have the stomach for it.

And for this particular dance style, I hear that's a bonus.

DINNER ON THE ISLAND

November 2003

When I recall my first visit to Mercer Island, I mostly think of Bob, friend of a friend of my dear friend's mother.

I confess that leaving my 480-square-foot condo in Belltown for a 4,000-square-foot home on Lake Washington takes a great deal of motivation on my part. I don't relate well to anyone needing so much floor space.

After a twenty-minute bus ride and a scary seat mate, we're over the floating bridge of I-90 and onto the island where I count eight Mercedes SUV's in a three block radius. This is bad, I think. It's obvious a Microsoft-of-the-nineties perspective still defines a sound economy on the island of means.

I don't know why suburbia scares me the way it does. And I'm not exaggerating. I am not even exaggerating. The feeling novocaines my enthusiasm and lives, ready to spring, inside my chest. And I know I'll spend the entire evening doing all I can to keep it there so it won't spring from my mouth. Which brings me back to Bob.

Six of us gather around a formally set table, where I suddenly feel plunged into an adult world I'm not privy to. After the salad is served (help, which fork to use?), Bob says he's disappointed the war hasn't turned the economy around. Bob, an unemployed "purchaser," was floored by the depressed high-tech computer industry. Apparently, there are no start-up businesses to purchase *for* in a time when Washington's unemployment rate is higher than the national average.

His words send me reeling. I think he is kidding. He is kidding, right? I look around. He is *not* kidding. And though the urge to scream comes over me and I want to drive his SUV through the holes in his logic, I try to choose my words carefully. There are a few social conducts I faithfully practice. Good social behavior at a dinner party is one of them.

Yet, there are times I'm not able to comply with my own code of ethics. When there *is* no code. When I simply can't (or won't) find the finesse to meet someone where they are. Instead, I need to catch them up to speed. My speed. "I can't believe I sat down to dinner with a man like you!" There. All control popped free. To my dismay, he laughs. The weird thing is, I sort of like him.

Still. How can someone who loves to garden, who baked a luscious cake for dessert—a tiered cake that wows us from a pedestal on the kitchen counter—feel so entitled as to be blase about war's toll on human life?

I can't find the pause button.

"Maybe the computer industry is not where you should stay," I say, wine-induced, fearless. "Turn to what you love. Become a chef! Could purchasing desks and phones be as gratifying as baking this fine cake?"

I look around. Everyone is staring down at his plate.

How will I find my way back to grace? Why, I wonder, is it so damn hard for me to get through an evening like this? I pipe up: "There have always been periods of economic shifting! It takes a willingness to risk to create change! You need to embrace the breakdown of the dot-com economy! Nothing changes if nothing changes!" All things I'd recently heard on NPR or read in the Evergreen Monthly, but whatever.

A silence falls over the room, a fine dusting of snow. I feel an urge to run. Thank god my hostess demands, with enough humor to make our standoff move from cold to warm, that it's time to sweep this conversation under the coffee table for good. And rightly so. She hasn't hired a caterer, she's done all the work of feeding us herself and doesn't need us stomping in combat boots all over her effort.

Later, in my kitchenette, I think about the fact that if character can be measured by what we say, and by what we don't, than I either had a lot of courage tonight or I was totally boorish, depending on which side of the issue you stand on. Still, exhausted on my bed which doubles as a couch, which doubles as my den, I feel a sliver of pride because even in an age of terrorism, I find this man's viewpoint the most scary of threats.

Lord knows I won't be going back to Mercer Island any time soon. What can I say? I'm a downtown girl. I might have acted less restrained than my dinner mates are used to, abandoning my manners like that, but I didn't abandon my conviction. I was not hollow. Besides, bad manners are something we do and then the drama is over. Conviction is a frame of mind with you *always*. And good to release now and again. Especially when things in never-never land need a little shaking up.

You just have to be ready for the little crash-of-chagrin that comes when it's over.

And to send an apology note to the hostess first thing in the morning.

EVERYTHING I NEED

December 2003

Yesterday, Thanksgiving. Today, drenched in obligation, Christmas!

How did an entire month accelerate faster than it takes to ride the monorail, and why doesn't my husband think so? To him the month dragged by. How is it that two working people sharing one home can experience the same bustling month so differently? Could the answer be that Christmas, like most celebrations, comes at a woman's expense?

In years past, in order to fulfill the obligations the season demands (my family is medieval Italian), I've focused as if on a finish line, adrenaline-amped, getting through the holidays rather than celebrating. Any initial rush of high spirits dissolved by expectation.

And last Christmas Eve, as a dear friend dropped off a gift without slowing down long enough to come inside, I remember thinking we exchanged gifts like change at a register, no time for the participation such finely wrapped boxes deserve. By January the season tapered off like smoke above my head, and relief is all I felt.

But, as I said, this season will be different. I won't do all of the "ought to's" (but I won't quite do none of them either). Just writing these words makes for an inner flush of calm. I refuse to worry if relatives think *Seattle's Best* coffee is a fitting enough gift, or that my mother-in-law won't appreciate the glass-blown Space Needle ornament. Or fret over the remote possibility that my old college roommate will visit, flirt the way she always does when she drinks, fall in bed with a Belltown bartender, leave her despicable husband, and move into the condo next door.

The problem is, despite my faith in the *spirit* of giving, I've lost patience for gift hunting and gathering. Save me from the disaster of all that guesswork. Lately, nothing I need or want, or want to give, can be wrapped up.

However, for the people who stood by me even when intimacy turned scary, our truest selves exposed, I promise to give more time, unconditional support, and gratitude. Especially to the man who could see our future together like another might see a board game many moves in advance, who convinced me to make room in my life to squeeze him in. And now the sheath that is us fits. He shows me every day how love can continue to grow like the philodendron that climbs our living room wall and trails through the sleeping loft. And like those humble vines, thank god we've found a way to creep over the biggest hurdles without tangling up.

Onward to a bright new year.

And before we know it, spring: the great thaw. Forsythia flaring yellow, too vivid to be true. Only it is true. Nothing cursory there.

THE SANDAL
January 2004

To reach this working class corner of Miami Beach you walk a mile north of the fashionable scene of South Beach. Then five blocks west to where real life zig-zags away from the Art Deco beachfront, glitzy and make believe as cubic zirconia.

I can't remember what the music transition is called when the bad thing is about to happen in a movie, still, it's the turn I hear as I walk up to the Starlite Bodega, where people rush in to buy beer, cream to protect them from the sun they seek, inflatable rings to keep their kids afloat. Because here, a girl stands with torn and ragged clothing, her foot with a missing toe like a gap between teeth, her terrified eyes like moons in the midnight of her skin.

I glance nervously at the man standing next to me. Through him I learn that these days when refugees wash up on the shores of Florida, it rarely makes the news. But they still come by the hull-full, and it's not unusual to walk the seafront at dawn and see a makeshift raft or crumbling rowboat beached on the sand.

By day two I can distinguish Cuban from Haitian, this refugee girl from those who arrived previously to clean hotel rooms. Who stand in white shirtwaists waiting for the bus.

As I turn to go, a woman walks up to the girl, a woman who reminds me of the squat, bleached-blonde mom on Jerry Seinfeld reruns: nasally whine, aqua-net hair, the clear sheet of vinyl I imagine covers her couch. And then the most appalling thing happens. The woman yells, "go home!" at the girl, whose whole body acquiesces, and I think, God, it's true: The most oppressed oppress the most.

And when a priest arrives, the girl smiles at him; each word he whispers is like a strand of silk eased over her skin. But when two policemen start to prod her into a van, fear, raw as a welt, turns her inside out. She vomits onto their shoes. Several people start to clap, and I can't stand back. I run up to her and for a moment she looks my way and all I can think to say is "I am so sorry."

Think of all the others adrift. Searching the Atlantic for this high-rise reef. Cane fields where they labor, machetes slashing their toes. Their lives, once they arrive, not as they pictured.

As for me: I'm a tourist from Seattle, bikini top and shorts, not yet hardened by these fringey streets. I haven't trained myself to pass obliviously, haven't developed an immunity to despair, know bigotry when I see it.

And when I see myself through the girl's eyes, I see a privileged white woman standing in a parking lot trying to apologize, which looks like doing nothing at all. Because that is exactly what it is. And then I see the tattered sandal she left behind.

I still can't put a name on that solitary shoe. Or the reverence I feel when it comes to mind. Reverence for a girl braver in her teens than I will likely manage in my life.

MEN, WOMEN & EARRINGS

February 2004

An unremorseful Valentine scrooge. That's what I am.

It's not that I don't consider myself romantic, but there's something undeniably cheesy about the weeks leading up to February fourteenth, little red hearts everywhere until we think buying something mushy is our own idea.

Yet, as long as we've been steered into the realm, I'll use the opportunity to say the best and most romantic way a man can show a woman he cares is to listen, *really* listen when she speaks. Can you imagine it?

Just yesterday, a friend confided to me that her well-meaning husband immediately latches on and tries to fix any problem she divulges. But what she'd prefer is what she and I share: a chance to brush fears away like bangs from our foreheads, to air grievances without the other moving in to rescue.

"Ah, but your husband isn't your girlfriend," I said. Call me vintage, but I think men are taught to be explicit from early on. It's what we oppose when we try to make them into our girl-pals. Men, at least the men I know, straight men anyway, don't feel the same need to yak, yak, yak about every small implication of a snag, a yen for intimacy behind each word. Their way of showing support is to try to solve the problem as one would a tear in a quilt. Which only adds insult to injury if a little connection is all you're after, not a solution.

I want to share a story pivotal to my understanding my husband, because the grown-up me needs to be reminded that marriage demands acceptance, patience wide as the land between oceans, and most of all, a well-timed sense of humor:

We'd just settled in for the evening to watch a movie where, in the opening scene, the female lead steps from the shower with two hoop earrings dangling from her ears. Before I go on, let me add that my husband thinks of me as sort of a prototype for women. And when I shower I remove my earrings, which, predictably, prompts him to say as if some gig between women was up, "Hey, she wore her earrings into the shower!" Bemused, I watch the rest of the film in silence.

Later, I ask him to name three things he thinks of when he thinks of women. His hesitation roams limb to limb. When he responds he is skittish, scared my breeziness will turn into a gale. "OK," he says, "Tears. How easily they come on." And it's true. When he tries to mend my fear as he would a leak in the roof, I can cry in frustration before going over it again: what women want, require, *long for*, is empathy, not help!

Then he adds "intuition." A potent internal scale, I agree, that balances two lives with devotion between them. Next, because, well, men will be men, he offers the word "breasts" like an unexpected gift, admitting they hardly warrant nicknames in a way that yoo-hoos my sense of humor back from its hiding place.

And, finally, with arms extended so we might finish this conversation unwounded, he says, "Earrings. You can bet they'll wear earrings."

PREJUDICE
March 2004

Just how is it possible to live so unmindfully?

This is the question I asked myself after a man offered to "pray for me" subsequent to my saying I can't understand anyone objecting to gay marriage in this day and age. I only wish I had challenged him out loud.

I lack comeback skills, an insufficiency that, early on, drove me to write. After a nasty set of "it" girls put Curlfree in my fifth-grade locker, writing was the only way I could express the humiliation I felt. They, of blonde hair and budding breasts, were everything a flat-chested, raven-haired girl—me—was not. And each possessed a mean streak I repeatedly confused with confidence.

Funny how, even now, with just a couple of disapproving remarks from a pious man, my self-assurance recoils. Part of me wishes I had given in to my first response, two hard syllables perched on the end of my tongue due to the fact I spent my formative years surrounded by Tonys and Marios in a working-class Italian neighborhood. This far west, I've learned to restrain my blasphemes (unless I'm really angry, disappointed, happy, or excited). Still, there are times when respectfulness is undeserved, especially when someone uses scripture to justify his own deeply held prejudices.

And pardon me, but I thought the Christian belief is, "God is love." Whenever two consenting adults propose to honor their love with a ceremony, it's a good thing for this alienated world. I wonder how people can fear gay marriage more than the monotony of a fearful mind?

As for me, when I entertain the notion of a God, I think more in terms of a mother figure multi-tasking like crazy to hold this wayward planet together. Frankly, I've met few men organized and compassionate enough for the job. Unless, a secretary and wife link him to these two qualities, staff any woman I know could surely use.

I'd like the man who offered to pray for me to ask himself three simple questions: "How would I feel if I were the recipient of this kind of judgment? What if I were gay? What if I was told my opinion needed saving?"

Perhaps the man thought I'd find him scrupulously superior. I didn't, of course. I found him obtuse.

When Boy George said "any love is good love," he changed my life. I was a kid and needing to hear that tolerance was possible. Though I lived in a "religious" home, my Roman Catholic family scorned anyone not conforming to their beliefs. I rushed out to buy the Culture Club album with titles such as: Love Is Love, Church of the Poison Mind, Do you Really Want to Hurt Me? I wanted to believe that things were really changing in the world and that acceptance would win the hearts and minds of most, even if, in our home, no mention of anything even remotely close to the word "homosexual" was ever uttered. I'm afraid this would still be true today.

For gay people, and basically any cause that tries to peel away layers of prejudice in order for people to live openly as they are, the problem is that we are more numb to violence than to dogma. And dogma wreaks fear, which is always a barrier between a real issue such as basic human rights, and the imagined catastrophe, such as all of civilization crumbling into a homosexual orgy.

Just think of the last time you needed to shift your life to accommodate something or someone because, even though difficult, you knew it was right. Remember the fear that kept you up at night? Remember how misguided it turned out to be?

MARCH

March 2004

Winter's over. Thank God.

To someone like me, now it's all about spring, all of the time.
I hold to the very sound of the word. When I say it, I see a
lighter me dancing on a sunny patio, string of red-chili lights
twinkling its rails, my closest friends with party dresses on.

And just as that image buds, every limb of me utterly in love
with Seattle again, it occurs to me that there is still April to
contend with, when the light broadens but the rain still jabs
you in the back, a give and take that proves just how long
time can take.

Over the last months, I've spent many a dark-by-five
evening lounging in sweat pants in front of the TV. Sweat
pants that, if held up to the light, a clear view of Jed Bartlett
can be seen through the seat of them. The worst part: watching a mindful man run the country while our real president
makes a nightmare of things. All this as I down another bowl
of buttered popcorn, a soft roll of flesh beginning to form pil-
low-like on my waist, enthusiasm locked in some kind of
internal storage.

Searching the Internet for clarity on what a weather disorder feels like, as if I don't already know, I read that the winter blues are caused by varying degrees of light reaching the pineal gland deeply embedded in the skull. When stimulated, this pea-sized gland secretes melatonin, which affects moods and energy levels. For relief: Get outside for at least twenty minutes a day, sans sunscreen, to absorb the light and vitamin D. One site even lists the benefits of a high-colonic, an extension of spring cleaning I hadn't thought of.

None of this information breaks new ground for me, but it's helpful to study the topic rather than react to it, even if excessive whining is the only remedy I choose in the end.

Meanwhile, my mother pooh-poohs my case of the blahs, employing her pet phrase, "This too shall pass." She's right, of course. As sunlight lengthens, I trust energy will spill again. And what follows is a ceremonial unplugging of the television and a massive housecleaning. Two annual attempts to bail winter over the side of me like sea from a skiff.

It's taken me years to admit that if I'm lucky enough to live in the luxury of rivers, rain, lakes and sea, gray skies come with the territory. I'm not affirming a platitude such as *you can't have a rose without thorns*, but as a reminder next time I ask myself the way I'd ask a Ouija board, "Whyyyyy do I live in the Northwest?"

I suppose, on some level, I've been afraid. Not of being able to accept the grayness, but that I don't *want* to, the image of a warmer/sunnier existence always in the back of my mind. Yet I don't wish to start my life over somewhere unknown. The thought of it exhausts this middle-aged me. Instead, I want to

want the life I've made and worked for. Even if I have to practice reacting favorably to the drizzle, as with any skill I've ever
been good at.

So it looks as though I'm faced with a tough attitude adjustment.

This morning, I try to become the new me. Wanting to or no,
I don't carp on the fact that sunlight doesn't wake me.
Instead, I focus on the glorious moment, right around noon
(or two or three), when the light finally pokes through and
I'm astounded by the lush pungency of earth renewing itself.

Add to that a flock of starlings turning at the same moment
in the sky, a sense of freedom I long to follow, which is more
than enough desire for one day if I'm to get any work done
whatsoever.

And with any luck, I figure the sharp edges between my predis-
position and the reality of where I live will begin to soften at last.

Of course, failure is also a possibility. And likely. Whenever I
confront a hard truth about my flawed self, I usually wind up
discovering something new to revise instead. That's when I
think that it's a good thing I gave it a go or I might have over-
looked the part of me most in need of fine tuning.

IV.

*"Please give me some good advice in your next letter.
I promise not to follow it."*

— Edna St. Vincent Millay

THANK YOU AND NOT SO
MUCH A THANK YOU

April 2004

I'd like to reply to some of the wonderful, and not so wonderful, mail I've received about my column, *A Writer's Notebook*,
since its first appearance in 2001. Until recently, I've not been
able to say "I am a columnist" with the same assurance I've
been able to say "I am a writer" or "I am a poet." And while I
can't say columns are all I write these days, they are a huge
part of my work and I get tremendous satisfaction from writing them. Even more from the fact that some people seem to
enjoy reading them. So I figure I've not only earned the title
'columnist' but the privilege of thanking my readers.

I'll begin with the positive feedback because it's easier to
express gratitude than to give words to the nameless malaise
that usually accompanies a bombast of dislike. (Six years later,
I'm much better at remembering that disapproval is only one
person's opinion, just as a column is.)

To my neighbor who thanked me for the poetry I included last
April, a poem dedicated to her son's life: I hadn't known my column ran five years *to the day* of his death, but it occurred to me
I might be doing some good by putting my take on things into
print, a good feeling for a writer to experience now and again.

To the woman who wrote that my column adds joy to her life: Thank you. Not only for the compliment but for the time it took to write a proper note. An act of generosity that still makes the cycle of giving complete.

To the man who dropped a line to say he reads my columns out loud to his wife, and to the woman who said my latest column is magnetized to her refrigerator (and she wasn't my mother), I give thanks. Acknowledgment awakens a writer's heart cell by cell.

To the Catholic priest who invited me to rejoin the church: I was touched by the gesture both tolerant and sincere, even if not tempted.

Okay. Now the icky stuff:

To the reader who asked me why I, a poet, am not embarrassed to be writing for a newspaper. That's easy. I've never belonged to the school that believes that a "true" poet writes only poetry or else commits an act akin to adultery. Elitism in any form makes me cringe.

Next, to the woman who wrote on behalf of "all good Christians" that my support of gay marriage is offensive: I've never understood how those who call themselves "children of God" can close their minds to what the other kids need.

To the man who called me "un-American," I have a question for you: How could we have back-stepped so far as to think that free speech is no longer the cornerstone of American privilege? Whose America do I stand for if not my own?

To the man who questions whether my essays are "worthy." Good God, I could never live up to a word like that. Trying to would squeeze the life right out of me. As for your other point that challenged my *opinions*. Bravo! Each of us is entitled to say what we think. (Unless, in my case, I'm thanking my mother for the last getup she sent me for Christmas.)

For the record, though, why would someone who is ostensibly free-thinking come down on an opinion? Maybe an action, but why an opinion? Because that's all a columnist is, someone paid to have an opinion. Or do you take issue only with ones you don't agree with? Because something about your tone reminded me of my father's voice back when my opinion was referred to as "talking back."

And lastly, to whoever scribbled that I write for my hometown newspaper because I could never swim in a larger pond: Well, well. You ought to do your homework. Workhorse that my immigrant background groomed me to be, I travel throughout this country (oh … and Europe) because of my work, and sometimes I'm paid a sum that makes champagne in order. Martinis if we're really talking. So let me ask you, how deep is your pond exactly?

Sidebar: I think my husband hit the nail more squarely on the head when he said that fault-finding is a kind of shared amusement amongst those who feel dissatisfied with their own lives. If your own calling remains unresolved, what's more comforting than kibitzing about so-and-so because that person is out there making what she wants exist, which can threaten those unable to do the difficult and humbling work of making things happen for themselves.

And lastly, to the postmistress in Chimacum who "totally relates to my column": I left your office with a smile on my face, a feeling that made me wonder if maybe, just maybe, I'm through with caring what others think of my work. What I mean is, I'm happy that some like what I write, and tell me so. Gratitude is always a healing tonic. And if they don't, well, I make no attempt to justify it.

EASTER EGG BREAD
(Pane di Pasqua all' Uovo) — for Jackie

April 2004

Every year around this time, as Easter rolls around and the first signs of spring blossom new wants as well as old hurts, one specific holiday rises up in mind, much like the dough my mother kneads to make her wreaths of Easter bread, punching with one fist, then both fists until three round balls are formed. In fact, whenever I think back over the vast energy of my mother's will to please on holidays, I can pinpoint this particular day in my mother's kitchen. It was 1973.

But I don't want to mislead you. I wasn't always so present in my mother's kitchen. It was a time of casting off aprons for all things bra-less, a metaphor of freedom I wore eagerly. I thought if I could shake off my mother's domesticity, I might find a daring life of my own, secretly fearing I didn't yet possess the delicate balance of confidence and resolve needed to do so. Not even close.

Anyway, that year, overlooking our bread ritual was my mother's new friend, Mrs. McKenzie, taller, richer, and more stylish than the women of my un-assimilated, working-class Italian family. Still, she had no better manners than to say she couldn't believe how much preparation *Eye-tal-yen* holidays take. My mother looked at me and I looked at her and we both cringed because there was no polite way to deny or correct her misuse of sound light-years from appropriate. Ahem, was all my mother managed to utter before she shrugged and changed the subject.

To our suburban Connecticut neighbors, my mother's kitchen served as the wood stove of an era past. It's where they circled to be warmed by loaves of just-baked bread. Our family brought an old-worldliness to a newly constructed cul-de-sac where dinner was more likely to be released from a can rather than prepared. Even in our most anonymous of suburbs, people will seek out a community, a place to engage with others, sensing that without it they're not connected to their surroundings in any real way. I mention this because it addresses a desire similar to the one I'm about to describe:

That day, before the neighbor women arrived, I watched my mother stand on a chair to remove the crucifix from our kitchen wall. My reaction was a mix of confusion and fear, a knot pulled tight inside me. And I strained to squelch it so it wouldn't turn into a gasp, tears, or especially a criticism. Still, it was the most hazy moment of dissolution I can remember from childhood, my mother's identity, and so my own, in absolute crises.

With a sweep of her hand, my mother removed the cross she refused to bear, a holiness she worried would be construed as old-fashioned. And with Jesus out of sight, our kitchen became a sudden, make-do version of modern.

A lifetime of rehashing later, I realize that ever since moving to the suburbs from the Italian-owned sidewalks my mother knew in the city, what she craved was to be unique and not provincial in her new neighbors' minds. For she believed, and rightly so, it made her special, all her cooking, the only competence that helped quell her deepest fear of inadequacy. And what she projected onto me was a fear that she was "less than," what so many immigrants and the children of immigrants have faced through the ages as they try to assimilate into a world more foreign than they ever imagined. In that moment, I learned what shame looks and feels like and how that bewildering emotion has made me do some pretty bizarre things throughout the years to try and fit in.

And anyone who knows my mother will tell you that much of her enthusiasm has always stemmed from food and the making of it, an activity that forces anyone in its throes to focus only on the present which rewards with its own level of satisfaction. To this day she is devoted to her Easter Egg Bread, a sweet braiding of dough dotted with pastel-colored eggs, a combination of recipe and skill I know better than to try to emulate.

But when my friend Jackie Leone, who found her way out of the Bronx and into a prosperous life on Seattle's Capital Hill, bakes the same Easter loaves, I long to be near them, their scent warm and familiar and deeply reassuring.

Actually, setting the bread aside, *everything* about Jackie is warm and familiar and deeply reassuring. I suppose there's another need to address here, an unrelenting fear of being this far west without anyone who reminds me of who it is I really am.

THE HERO
May 2004

In Port Townsend, on Water Street, I lean into the window of a gallery, admiring a painting that is so true, it leaves me breathy with optimism, as if the artist wants to shed light because that's who she is. Nothing prepared me for the honesty it impressed upon me.

I don't know why things occur as they do. Let me say that another way. I have absolutely no clue why things occur as they do. But some chance events are more assuring, more illuminating than others.

So, here I am on the sidewalk, all this reassurance reaching in, when an old acquaintance, Richard, walks by, which is hardly an unlikely coincidence during the Rhododendron Festival, when our county congregates en masse, accelerating toward whatever it is the eldest festival can promise the nostalgic heart of a fast-growing, overpriced, tourist town.

There is no pretending. Our eyes meet. Try as I might, I can't turn away.

These days, I'm inclined to smile at someone holding a slice of my past in their hands. But if we share nothing of the present,

I don't feel the same need to stop and catch up. Everything fades with time, and I've rounded the corner of feigning interest if I have none. It's not a corner exactly, more of a gradual surrender, but the point is the past can feel like such an anchor, partly grounding, partly holding me back. Because I'm never sure just how much the conversation will require to get us through to the present, which is where I prefer to be.

But he walks closer and laughs a familiar, songful laugh I remember so well. Really, he perfects the art of the laugh, and, in spite of my preference, which now looks down on me, mockingly, we proceed to catch up on the last decade we'd lived through, though separately.

Lastly, we find our stumbling way into Iraq because, I suspect, he too, cannot play this down and leave it in our background like the snowy peaks of the Olympic mountains. He clears his throat. Looks around. Then he says that, as a decorated Vietnam hero, he never did a goddamn thing to deserve to be honored. That the only thing he ever did even *close* to heroic is to speak up. He wasn't defending his country, he was trying to stay alive, that's all, and he was full of rage for having to fight a war he had no understanding of. Rage is what he took out on the Vietnamese people. Pure, fucking rage. And I quote, "Mostly when I was high."

His admission stuns me into silence. Bless him for relieving us of the pretense that can surround the subject of patriotism as of late.

"There are two kinds of soldiers," he adds in a tone indicating he has clearly spoken these words before, "The ones afraid to speak up. And the ones court-martialed if they do."

I believe, like the painting before him, he was put in my path to enlighten me.

As to the horrifying photos of masked Iraqi prisoners, he said point-blank: "We are naive to think we can train our troops for war, send them off to fight a war, then expect they won't act warlike. War is always horrifying. I can't even begin to describe the insane brutality of it."

"As for Bush," he added, "history will condemn his right-eousness."

I too, believe this will happen. Perhaps years from now, but it will happen. Of course, I say this with more sureness than I feel.

In an absolute worst-case scenario, he'll be elected again.

THE SUMMER PEOPLE
July 2004

I'm quite sure, if given the opportunity to travel right now, I'd swallow the chance whole, wrap up this essay and hightail it to the airport.

Instead, nose to the grindstone with a deadline to meet, I'm fully envious of the woman next door. A woman who is relaxed and reading in a lawn chair. And hours later when I rise from my computer to stretch, she'll still be there. And while tourists stroll by my Port Townsend cottage, staring with longing, wondering if our way of life might carry them to the next best place in their own, my envy grows.

Before I go on, I should explain that at some indeterminate point between my last book of poetry and this collection of essays, I became far more interested in this stream of passers by. Oh hell, I've taken to eavesdropping to afford me grace periods of laughter between the waves of vulnerability writing a book instills in a writer. And since there is barely a pause between our commerce-driven festivals these days, the increased foot traffic allows me to feel in the mix rather than the sediment that sits here writing about it.

Granted, my ability to snoop is enhanced by the fact that in front of my home, three bronze poetry plaques rise from my garden like stations of the cross, while my office, only a few paces from the sidewalk, is hidden by a colossal holly tree. This is one of those unique coincidences that makes life fascinating! On the rare occasion when someone says something I can't resist writing down, I am extremely happy.

I realize that this all sounds nosey and foolish, not to mention imprudent, but having sat in this office though six books and two decades, I can say that despite all I've gained in assurance, discipline, and the ability to stay in my pajamas until 3 p.m. without the slightest guilt, I seem to have lost something in the way of correctness, politically or otherwise. Spy and snoop, this is what fun has become.

The Family:

They look like any suburban family on holiday: shorts, billboard T-shirts, Teva sandals, cameras-as-accouterment. The conventionally-casual look of American tourists everywhere. A look that causes me to go limp with boredom.

What the parents say to each other makes me cry out "ha!" which startles the family flock.

Woman: "People here are kind of artsy."

Man: "Yeah, but they could still water their lawns."

Woman: "The gardens are lovely."

Man: "Well, what else is there to do around here?

Two Women:

I'd wager they are attending the writers conference.

Steady yourself, I'm not kind here: One wears a loose, layered, au naturel ensemble, the ghost of clothing past. As if to say, "I live in my head for I am l-i-t-e-r-a-r-y." The thing is, it reads more as, "I live in 1969 for I am s-t-u-c-k."

And you know how sometimes women tease, back comb, and spray their hair until it looks as if it will stand up to a Port Townsend wind? Is she from Texas, I wonder, or Wenatchee?

Woman in Layers: "Do you think that's the poet sitting in there?" Meaning me.

Big-Hair Gal: "Well, she *must* do something other than write poetry; this is the high-rent district."

On a good day, I just listen. On a bad day, an *annoying* day, I reply in a voice that is ninety parts Roseanne Barr, ten parts my mother.

Two Teenage Girls:

Teenager No.1: "Hey, you want to read these poems?"

Teenager No. 2: "Yeah, right."

The Couple:

I hear the woman's shoes on the sidewalk as my cat hears a dog's chain jingling from two blocks away. She wears those strapless heels my friend Rachel calls "clickers," and black-rimmed glasses that pronounce one's urbaneness as if with a gavel. Painstakingly coiffed head to toe, her look is more paid-for than is common around here. Tailored rather than ass-in-hiding.

Her partner's presentation is a bit more—I'm trying for the verbal description—gone to seed. Flannel shirt torn off at the elbows (!) and a ponytail that falls from the back of his balding head in a gray, midlife-in-denial strand. Definitely boat festival. Sea shanty-esque. And he is at least twenty years older than she. It *so* bothers me they are holding hands.

She: "Do people live here year-round?"

He, with a thick (is it Maine?) accent: "Silva spooners. Olda folks. Ahtists. Writas. Hippies who want to live fah from the city."

His comment would have been funny, had it not been true. As they walk on he says, "Let's find All-Driches Mahket."

For the first and only time, I'm glad the store burned down.

The Man With MSAIHKWHITAS (Male Speaking As If He Knows What He Is Talking About Syndrome):

He informs his wife that the reason the incline of the Haller Fountain steps is so gradual, steps that lead from downtown to our uptown residential neighborhood, is because people's legs in olden times were frailer. Come again?

Really, could there be anything more annoying than an untruth stated as fact? It cuts a swath through my sense of humor. I want to stand, walk outside, and read aloud from the poem on the plaque in front of him:

111

You can't help but think
of pomposity
when you walk the Haller Fountain stairs
once made of wood, the diminutive, aristocratic steps
you must take on your way up
so proper gentlewomen could hike
the hem of their dress ankle-high and climb
ladylike to a prosperous summit.

But there is another element to this admission, a pressing need that I don't fully grasp at first and that, even now, I can only admit sort of reluctantly: I have way more emotion than I ever anticipated tied up in my writing, and I want, no I expect, this man to read my words and to *get* it! Better stated, I might be impossibly attached to my writing the way others are to their children with unmitigated pride: Don't you see how my words (kids) are special. Sometimes this delusion wears me out completely.

Left with this thought, I don't say a word. Instead, I sit here focusing on two bugs nosing my windowpane, queen of self-restraint, losing my will and gaining sufferance, what maturity feels like, I guess.

If it is, then I need to add this: I can't live up to it always. I won't.

SO MUCH ABOUT SUMMER
August 2004

As some of the longest, lightest days of the year fall off behind us, I feel, as most North Westerners do, that I positively must take delight in whatever remains of summer.

And there is so much good about summer in Seattle, the season I love to love, that frankly, I don't know where to begin.

So here's my best try: The first thing I did when I moved to Seattle on a balmy summer evening two decades ago was drive to Alki Beach. While daylight still beamed at nine p.m., I headed for the sand to see the end of the day slip into sea, sat on the flattest log until the sun, no longer round, sank below the horizon.

In this city, on the rare occasion when heat lingers into dusk, one indisputable pleasure, and to my mind the greatest pleasure, is to eat dinner outside. Best when freshly mown grass swamps your toes and a cat sprawls on your heat-soaked deck. Tonight behind a friend's West Seattle bungalow, engulfed in the wings of a wicker armchair, I do just that. And then I return to where there are plenty of reasons to give thanks for being on this earth: Alki Beach. By far the summery-est night of the season, there is something else I love about the mild air:

no wind. Which means a girl can walk on the beach and still have good hair, hair that behaves. It is a beautiful evening. A beautiful, *beautiful* evening. I could almost believe in God. Surely a Goddess.

Alki Beach has its rules: no cruising, no car stereos booming; I have mine: wear slip-off mules for easy exit, never *ever* press a cell phone to my ear, pretend I'm still impressed by the size of a crow if a tourist needs me to be.

In no time I'm swept up by the beauty of this place. A night like this with a clear view of the city, the ferry to Bainbridge gliding serenely by, and so much sea in the distance makes the rest of everything seem promising. Never underestimate the influential power of sand beneath your feet.

Why is it that whenever life picks me up like this, I must decide, right off, to stay lifted? My well-being at once something to seize rather than savor before some worry moves in or worse, snow-balls, causing me to wonder if one has failed at something even for a very short span of time in the grand scheme of living, will failure-fears nip at her confidence forever?

Here is where I have to decide to let nothing sabotage the veil of satisfaction between me and the world just now. Not the third dog to nose my gender, or its amused owner crouching but not grabbing his stinky dog away. Or two teenagers curled around each other with such innocent need it makes my heart ache. *Or* the intoxicated couple trading obscene insults, beer cans wedged between their legs, rising with a push and shove but not before it looks as if the woman is about to kill some-one. The man beside her, surely.

I look around for the intervention I am sure I'll find from the onlookers, but all I see is unconcern, reminding me that I can either read this couple's behavior as a monkey on my back, or else as relentless fortitude on the part of mother nature. It's all up to me.

And though the urge to run back to my car comes over me along with that blurry sense of alienation I feel whenever I see some meaningless violence filling the world, I wait, holding to my square of sand until the couple resorts to two drunken snorts of laughter and most people are gone.

Finally relishing the steady swish of waves lapping waves, the city pauses for a breath. One of those moments when all reverence is held within.

Nearly midnight, I finally stand, flinging sand from the seat of my pants. But only because I feel the beginnings of raw, crisp air off the sound, suspended between what is merely chilly to my skin and the downright cold that, even on the warmest night in our Emerald City, clearly comes next.

BURYING LILY
August 2004

It's appropriate, isn't it, that no formality exists around the burying of a cat or dog? Because, frankly, the few times I've heard of someone (other than a child) organizing a pet funeral, I've thought the whole idea absurdly American, the kind of ceremony only those with too much time and money on their hands could contrive. Especially with all the larger griefs that befall us.

Well, that was then. Before I lost my cat, a feline that held the locus of my affection in her paws, and suddenly equating my sadness to a greater sorrow doesn't lessen my own a bit. How unrealistic it is to compare heartbreaks.

The funny thing is, I didn't want a cat. I don't even own a house plant. I'm passionately devoted to my husband, my work, a few family members I can tolerate, and enough friendships to sustain me. In terms of commitment, this feels ample for me. But the cat arrived at my doorstep impossibly thin, ribs showing vividly through mangey fur, nothing subtle about her despair. So, as most would, I found a saucer and nourishment to fill it.

From there our fondness developed. It was around this time I started to repeat the words, "when you plant a seed and water it, it grows," inspired by the simplicity of the sentiment. And, of course, I was falling for the cat in a big way. Actually, I was all in. And beginning to wonder if I have any say over my emotions at all.

First, she slept in the woodshed. Then, in the laundry room. After that, every nook of our house became home to her soft, warm weight.

Looking back, I see how she was a relief in our lives, a calm departure from political chaos, wise in her own unruffled way. In her eyes, a clear message that life goes on no matter what. And at times I'd feel such a sting of affection I would scoop her right out of a curve of sleep just to squeeze her hard.

I also began to talk about her in the way new mothers can't help but turn every conversation back to the baby, which was getting to be a wee bit pathetic. And nights when I couldn't sleep, I'd reach for her warmth. Not the best for a marriage, I admit. But I thought of us as two females in need of a little comfort as we tried to drift off to the roar of snoring made by the only male in the house.

Then the inevitable day when there is no denying that the ultimate responsibility of owning a pet goes beyond helping it to live and accelerates into aiding its death. The day when you feel your insides are never going to be big enough to contain such sorrow.

I am first to admit I cared for my animal in ways that only the privileged of this world are able to. Her kitty-gourmet was nearly fifteen bucks a bag! Even so, I sensed things quickly escalating beyond my sense of propriety as soon as the veterinarian began naming options for her treatment: steroids, chemotherapy, exploratory tests, surgery. Not only was it the expense that stopped me, but the absurdity it felt like in contrast to what I feel is just and appropriate care for a pet. Even my pet.

My instinct was simpler. I bought a piece of floral fabric to wrap my cat's body in. I held her while she was anesthetized. I watched my husband dig a hole in the ground and cried a flood tide of tears before placing her in the earth with my own hands.

Putting any body, still warm from living, into the ground immediately puts many things into perspective. In the weeks following, I was amazed to find how easy it was to make a few decisions I'd put on hold for lack of clarity. And I found myself being acutely honest with people about all sorts of things. No holding back. (I'm still paying for that, by the way.)

As they say in New York, "Get over it, and if you can't get over it, get over talking about it."

This might sound harsh, particularly to the highly sensitive, but I remember the very morning I woke and thought, "That's it, not one more word about the cat!" And you know, it worked. My pain dissipated pretty quickly after that.

I don't regret that I allowed myself to love an animal so much. I believe the adage that says the biggest risk we can take in terms of love is not to take one. For what love isn't entwined with pain? The risk of loving is always about opening yourself up to the most vulnerable part of yourself, the precise feeling that connects us to the human race, the very defenselessness that makes the life-cycle complete. Oh! This is the thought I've been trying to express this whole time.

Who knew how much insight a tiny animal could arouse?

LOOKING BACK ON THE SUMMER OLYMPICS

September 2004

Ever since the Summer Olympics in Athens, I've been mulling over a few things about the games that made my hair stand on end. Nothing about the athletes, mind you. I could easily watch more of their grit and discipline: the gymnasts, the swimmers, and whatever those athletes are called who throw the discus and javelin.

Before I go on, I should explain the origin of this mull-over: How it began at the airport. How nothing quite matches the limbo-like feeling of an unscheduled layover. And yet, being forced to sit is a luxury of sorts, a chance to read an issue of *The New Yorker* cover to cover, the in-depth stories that remind how misinformed you can become if mainstream reporting is your only source of news.

The compelling article I came across described in detail the more seamy, behind-the-scenes practices of the Olympics. It made the outlandish TV commentary seem, ta da, exactly what it was: a spin.

But I don't blame the networks. Americans need something affirmative to feel good about these days. Still, that Bob

Costos, he's always good for a laugh. Two days into the games, he was touting the women's Romanian team as "one, big gymnastic family," causing my patience to short-circuit, "Family?" I yelled back at him. "They don't live with family. They live in gold-medal custody!" Granted, the confrontation didn't require much courage on my part; it was more of a maternal outburst, a rush of female-protecting-female in a world where women are inherently different from men.

In my rush to support the pitiable, rather than applaud the American team, I pulled for the Romanian women. Wait a second, they are *not* women. They are girls, removed from their families at the age of six, allowed a visit from parents only twice a year. Girls who are promised for each gold medal a bonus of $50,000, which in Romania is lifelong financial security, free rent for their families, and a car. Imagine the pressure on a preteen nervous system?

I am not arguing that money is not a good incentive. But surely something honorable is lost when gold-medal inducements are so far out of proportion to what any civilized nation should ask a child to live for. And it's why the next evening I cheered for the American gymnast, Carly Patterson, delighted when she won the all-around gold. It wasn't only a pang of patriotism. I wanted the young athlete to prove to the world that a child can see her mother and father daily, eat enough to develop properly, and still be a self-disciplined winner.

But even more outlandish than what occurs behind the dazzling panorama of the games are the ad campaigns between contests, promotion tactics that always stop me cold if I haven't watched a television in a while. I suppose it's successful advertising if it sways us to tune in with a bad case of what a friend calls FOMS (fear of missing something). But to my mind, the makers of the Hummer, the worst gas-guzzling, ego-machine ever, should not be allowed to be a "proud sponsor of the Olympic games." Proud? Of *what*, pray tell?

Yet something else in the magazine article offers a small, playful comfort and is a huge reminder that long before there were advertising agencies or gold medals, there were the Ancient Greeks and the original medieval games, when only male athletes competed in the nude while only men were allowed to watch.

Like most women, I read into this what I already know is true, that the world has been about men for men's sake for a very long while. But leaving that thought on the peripheral, ooh la la, the image does entice does it not? Forgive if I overstate, but I don't think any present-day promoter of the games would be willing to remember history as it really was and what the first games were really meant to boost and strengthen.

Cross a mental threshold and conceive of the kind of tolerance this ad campaign could bring to our sports arena. And so, to our lives. It might sound crass, but it's true. And doesn't the truth always make for a better world?

THE RIGHT SIDE OF THE PLATE
October 2004

I'm still not sure why I accepted another dinner invitation on Mercer Island, home to the oh-so-wealthy. I should have trusted my instinct that passed in a heated rush from my stomach into my throat soon as I heard the hostess's voice on my answering machine. I waited for my hand to reach for the receiver to extend my apologies, knowing full well I wasn't brave enough to do so.

Now, looking back over the evening, I think not so much of the lovely things: the awesome view from the living room or the impossibly plush carpet beneath my feet, but how marriage is about fairness, and this particular night was no exception.

The host of the dinner party, my husband's associate, is a lawyer. Also present was the lawyer's associate, also a lawyer, and their wives who, by what I could gather, make careers out of their children's likes and dislikes. Five kids and two dogs between them, I agreed to go only because the next night my husband and I were headed to *Assagio's*, my favorite downtown restaurant, to dine with an Italian from the Bronx, which means the pace of our conversation would accelerate past my husband's ability to comprehend it, and later, we'd stop by an underground music studio belonging to Elaine, an irreverent, snazzy star of her own rock and roll band. Essentially, *my* friends.

On to the aim of my story: In my circles, people are hoping (praying!) for a better direction for our country after the election. But sometimes all it takes is a social evening away from my tribe to remind me how buttoned-up the world can be outside the familiar borders of my world.

Perhaps there is truth to the new-age prophecy that the one outcome you fear most is the one you will create. Or is it that you can expect the best or fear the worst? *Or* that your deepest struggle will produce your greatest whatever it is, the point is that the one thing I dreaded most about the evening, Artsy-Fartsy-With-No-Kids-Meets-Conventionality, settled down to grow. As soon as we arrived, I knew my clothes were completely wrong, not suburban enough, but more conspicuously out of place was my sense of humor, my directness, my verve. Some attitudes just don't travel well from downtown to the islands. *Help me Rhonda, help, help, me Rhonda*, I muttered alone in the bathroom, *HELP ME Rhonda, yeah, get me out of this place.*

I know small talk is the medium of the dinner party but I have little patience for it. Life is too short for safe topics. I'm not afraid of verbal mistakes. Neither are the people I like to socialize with. Blunders are part of the process, part of the foolishness that gets you to the center of the thing you are trying to say. It's the same mental process I go through every day, so to me, the fumbling doesn't seem like a lack of articulation the way it will around a table with men whose time is measured, itemized, and billed in six-minute segments.

Besides, if I'm going to go through the work of communicating, I want to be in the company of people who think out loud willingly so that even the uncomfortable things come rolling off our tongues in a gut-longing for truth. Which is why we can make a polite, dinner party hostess giddily nervous.

And beware of conversations between moms and me that begin innocently enough. Sooner or later the essence of the Difference Between Us comes crashing in, and in this case, it's why our dinner group's exchange about bicycling deteriorated pretty quickly into a crossfire:

When asked if I wore a bike helmet by one of the other women, I tried to explain my love for wind in my hair, but before my words could sprout, she interrupted with what I can only describe as that disciplinary "mommy" voice. Here we go, I thought, one American policing another, liability issues the end-all power ploy. Sure enough, she went off about the high cost of medical treatment once my skull is cracked open. *Oh come on.*

So here's my question: Why is it socially acceptable to be criticized for not wearing a bike helmet but lord help me if I were to point out a few particulars about her physique that might inevitably cost a chunk of change in terms of heart disease and diabetes?

Cocktail-woozy, we sat down to dinner, by then relying on the possibility the evening might improve in proportion to the number of empty wine bottles between us. I'd already been labeled the liberal-at-the-table, so why upset the vox populi? For an opener, I brought up Teresa Heinz Kerry. By now the words *acting out* could well apply.

"What about Teresa's speech at the Democratic Convention? How brave was she, huh, to flat-out say that men are thought of as smart for voicing strong views, while a woman is labeled *opinionated*, a word with a thousand degradations tacked to it?" Maybe I was hoping for a conversation about our presidential campaign, how it's evolved to where we vote for the wife as well as the man, but in retrospect, you and I both know that's not true.

If I once thought only men found women like Teresa Heinz Kerry threatening, I stand corrected. The other women seemed put off by her candor. And I won't delve into all the self-esteem issues this conjures up.

It's an election year. The truth had to surface. Both couples were voting for Bush. And when they nodded in agreement that the Middle East has to be "handled," I wondered what "handled" means to people who use the word so easily. Do they mean like how my silverware is lined up before me or how my salad plate belongs on the right of my dinner dish?

Okay, I thought, I can handle this. But the delicate balance we tried to maintain between staunch them and staunch me was pretty shaky throughout the rest of the evening, a turf war of our own, insufferableness blocking any sophistication on either side. And it didn't help any that, in my host's opinion, my political orientation was tantamount to burning the flag or, at the very least, to dropping my blue jeans right there on his living room floor.

Someone wise once said, "A bad dinner party is good training for the rest of your life."

Well then, apparently, I've received excellent training. Because I've had, what, two maybe three invitations to dinner since Bush was elected? Each disastrous. But I'm not sorry for my obstinance. I accept the blame.

This seems a good time as any to establish a rule of thumb about where I should venture between now and November second. Because I wish I had the confidence to say I could get through the next couple of months without a single confrontation, but I'm afraid the breach between "sides" is so wide all courtesy has fallen through.

And perhaps that's not such a bad thing when the issues are this difficult to face, not because the problems are complex, though they are, but because neither side will listen to the other. So we have no choice but to *make* each other listen.

That's really a loaded word, *make*. And more than a little scary.

So much for patience and tact.

DAY AFTER THE REELECTION

November 3, 2004

8 a.m.

Here's something I never expected: For the first time in my sun-loving memory, I prefer clouds. Ominous and weighty clouds. Clouds that mirror my darkened mood. Crushed, actually. *Crushed* mood. Surely, this is how the writer must have felt before coining the phrase "the dark ages."

8:30 a.m.

Fear-stunned, the news knocks over the worried mess of me. I keep flinching.

9:15 a.m.

I will myself not to cry. And to reclaim the present: the sunlight, my office, this essay.

9:20 a.m.

Tears. And by no means are they wimpy, whiny tears. They are an explosive what the fuck is happening? flood tide of rage-filled tears. Optimism has deserted me.

9:25 a.m.

Mind you, the light will return.

9:30 a.m.

War. War. *War*. I'm sick to death of thinking, talking, writing what hurts too much.

10 a.m.

Still, I won't cave like my friend who says, in order to get through the next four years, she'll have to join the long line of antidepressant-poppers.

10:30 a.m.

I think about the passage my husband read to me last night while I waited for sleep, words from a book about Magellan's circumnavigation of the globe. It went something like, "How corrupt our government, how it lies to its people and steals its power from the opposition. How grief is always a partner of change."

I keep running the lines, written so long ago, hoping perspective is a muscle strong enough to hold me together.

This election is not the crumbling of the moon or the shattering of the sun.

11:30 a.m.

I know when faced with the reality that part of the world wants to attack you and is willing to die doing so, most will turn to the safe habits of patriotism and religion, things that sound morally admirable on the surface but decimate underneath, like the underside of a trimmed lawn, composting behind a good front.

What I mean is, I know and I don't know.

12 p.m.

I've tried to remain calm, level-headed, forward thinking. But you know how it feels when there is this potency within that needs to vent?

How am I to understand Christians who condone war and yet despise a ceremony of love between gay men and women? Our president shows by example that it is okay to lie, strong-arm, judge, condemn and invade, to put religious zeal in front of the real issues of poverty, education, and health affordability.

And abortion is not one of the issues; we already decided that. I can hardly bare the thought of men from a congregation stiff and hard as the pews they build, so isolated from the way I live my life, making moral decisions for women.

So, here's what I think: When obtuse leaders think they know all, we had better be ready to wade in the aftermath of tyranny. And to accept it on some level if we can, because we have to since we won't be able to stop thinking about it.

12:05 p.m.

A lump of dread pounds double-time.

My editor will totally reject this column. But even if I wanted to revise this, which I don't, my fingers tap away on their own. Brave, my fingers. Nimbly hoping against hope.

12:15 p.m.

By the age of twelve, I could no longer buy the insult of "Virgin Mary" and wondered how my mom, the mother of three, *could*.

I feel the same disbelief now about the right-to-lifers; how smug in their moral superiority they are. How can any thinking woman willing to take responsibility for her life belong to any fold wanting to take that very duty away from her? Is this how we are taught to value ourselves?

I didn't know just how much was pent up.

Now I do.

12:30 p.m.

I wait to feel a certain shift in the air. As if it's all been a horrible mistake in order to scare the apathy out of us.

So far, nothing. With a mean streak.

Denial kicks in: Surely both the left and right, sensing our country sliding into a downward spiral, will decide to work together and render us better than before. Right?

1 p.m.

In the first place, why do we support any country where women are treated no better than dogs?

Talk about a polarized country. The night before the election, I had a screaming match with my seventy-eight-year-old mother: *Mom, it is possible, simultaneously, to support our country and detest the men who are running it!*

1:15 p.m.

So now I feel entirely not up to the task of balancing on the high wire of family dynamics the upcoming holiday season will demand of me, the presence of mind it will take to communicate as equal adults to the same people who brought me into this world and held my hand as I stumbled through it. I haven't the backlog of patience to manage dealing with parents and siblings who can still push those tender buttons inside me that, as much as I hate to admit it, can return me to adolescence or a further regression, a toddler on all fours.

This year, unfortunately, the button is politics, so heavy on our minds all of this.

THE SCENT OF HOLIDAY

November 2004

Why is it that, when I inhale certain fragrances, I am, pow, all at once transported back in time?

I really can't say. Scientifically, that is. The only thing I'm certain of is that everything that defines "holiday" for me will stem from a scent, a whiff of food that will wedge a memory from the inner folds that make up my life.

Which isn't to say that all remembering is lighthearted. Sometimes the only thing that stands between a scent and recollection is pain, when inhaling will hurt far more than hearing or seeing. And the ache doesn't alter with the passing years. Something so real never changes one bit. Or becomes otherwise.

One inhale of a simmering pot of tomatoes that is to become sauce that is to become a lasagna and my family is moving from the crowded streets of our inner city Italian neighborhood to the spacious suburban dream: a split-level house at the end of a New England cul-de-sac, lawns suddenly level as the sidewalks we left behind. Where it took only one nightfall to grasp how dark nighttime really was. And that my toys could stay outside and no one would steal them. To a city kid this was *big*.

"We're moving up!" my father proclaimed. "Up to where?" I wondered. A child's life is so literal.

My mother's response was to cling. To custom. Her family had left behind Italy for New England's version of Little Italy, and then, three daughters in tow, she left the city for the suburbs. Cooking was her lifeline. So while the kids in my new school ate bologna sandwiches homogenized as the mayonnaise that soaked them, I spooned Pasta Fagioli out of a steamy thermos. What was once my favorite meal now horrified me. I took to throwing my lunch away rather than suffer the taunting that pasta and peppers would surely attract.

As memories go, this is a pretty easy one to dredge up. And doing so has brought about another: The smell of garlic will forever remind me of the cloves my mother peeled and chopped by hand until her Ball jar was brimming. To this day, all of me comes through that smell in a pang of guilt because I would never, *ever* help her. I didn't want my fingers to smell like hers, the odor accompanying her wherever she went. Now I realize it wasn't help she needed so much as a presence to ease the solitude her days had surely become in contrast to apartment living. She owned a larger, more dazzling home, yes. But in all ways that matter to a woman used to family, company, and neighborhood chatter, a smaller life.

And if that isn't enough of a guilt trip, one sniff of the pungent bulb and my father is praising "the old country," causing me to roll my eyes and run off, palms pressed to my ears. Like the language he spoke, his history was too alien to be my history. I didn't want to think about the past. What child does? In a matter of a few suburban weeks, I'd migrated from the emotional culture of my family to that of Middle America.

This is not an easy thing to write down, that mixed with every waft of garlic is not only the arrogance of youth but the presence of a glacially slow process of self-forgiveness as I find my way back to the current me, a humbling process that needs to plow through layers of chagrin.

Funny how time does change everything. Yesterday my mother's efforts gave way to my own: I minced enough garlic to fill a jar. Eventually, once I got through the discomfort it roused, I felt completely at ease, a feeling I wish I could get at more often. And when my husband asked how long it took to chop so much garlic by hand, it occurred to me the answer had little to do with minutes or hours: "A lifetime," I said.

Remorse, with its power to unhinge me, pretty much gone.

'TIS THE SEASON
December 2004

What happened to the exhilaration I used to feel around the holidays? Anticipation so possessed I ached with it. Where did those feelings go?

Does the answer exist only on an emotional level or was my enthusiasm fueled by real things such as our house trimmed gaudily, even the yard tricked out until it looked like Mardi Gras come home to roost in our New England cul-de-sac? Or my mother in her finest dress so that, to a child looking up, sequins on satin were like stars in the sky? Or the feast she'd lay out, food that is still our family's way of reconnecting to our past selves as opposed to who we've become.

I still can't imagine myself staging such extravagant meals, such gusts of readying, my mother holding still only long enough to serve the food, talk about the food, or to accept a compliment lavished on the food.

And even though I try to uphold a few of our food traditions, corralling ingredients until they're ready to burst from my fridge, recreating the same level of child-like glee just isn't possible. Which can leave an enormous void between the expectations of the holiday and what it actually delivers. For a start, as children we aren't responsible for the details of festivity, for the work and stress of it. And the blatant truth of grownup-ness is that we have to work hard for *everything*, celebration included.

And once December rolls around, the weeks ahead can wreak havoc on my vulnerabilities, which can leave me in a beastly mood. When old griefs or disappointments return, I can either blame the holidays for my melancholy, or mourn each sadness one-by-one.

Granted, it'd be wonderful if images of family bliss were still part of my family's scrapbook, but the reality of my present-day family is not as cozy as all that. And writing about it doesn't make easier the fact that what once seemed like too many miles separating us grew into too many differences causing me to disengage round about Thanksgiving rather than connect, the result of living one kind of life while the media imagines I lead another. Even if I promise myself I won't be seized by the ravages of holiday nostalgia, it's a landmine of emotions I prefer to be done with straightaway. If not sooner.

But don't read me wrong, I haven't thrown in my towel on festivity altogether, even if there has been a shift in expectation. In fact, I'm throwing a whopping Christmas party. And anyone who has ever delighted in one of my parties will tell you that if dependence-on-celebration were illegal, I'd be found guilty of living under the influence of shimmy-dancing in a to-die-for dress, martini in hand, hugging my friends while we sway side to side in perfect tenderness. As my favorite saying goes, "I may not be a celebrated writer, but I am a writer who celebrates." Enough to remind me what it is I need to feel in terms of joy every now and again if I'm to feel settled in this world.

Still, there's another reason I want to throw this party: Lately I'm bored with what passes for one. All of us standing around, clinging to cocktails, composed and smiling, chit-chat mingling in the air. No one giving in to full-bellied gaiety until I, too, am numbed into submission, behaving properly. Ugh!

I suppose the fact that I'm a dancer is why, at my Christmas party, we won't sing tedious carols. Instead, I'll turn up the Motown and coax my guests into cutting loose with a little hip action, until dance-abandon is pried loose. I prefer the emotional release of a good boogie to the intricacies of someone's troubles if I'm all dressed up and waiting for a party to lift off. The gift of a party should be two things: that we feel safe enough to grab hold of our fun selves. And to focus only on the present.

Because just think of all the pleasure we give up while waiting for something elusive as "happiness." Or, worse, security. No matter what any journalist (what do they know?) says, we have it better now then ever. It's obvious we enjoy the highest standards of living in the world so why don't we revel in appreciation of that fact each and every day? Or, at least when we gather together to supposedly celebrate. I figure if I don't experience some kind of euphoria in December, how will the January blues, sure to set in soon as the tree lies face down in the compost, inflict its proper effect?

I'll wrap this up by sharing what happened last time I went to a party where people attended, yes, but did not do the work of participating. I'm not exactly proud of my reaction, but I'm hardly ashamed of it either.

You know how good it feels when you think some real fun just might happen? I walked into the party like that, with spirits high as my heels. And then the gut-wrenching reality of what the night would be, or what it would not be as I stood in a festively decorated home in a swarm of people preoccupied with a discussion about real estate and interest rates, party talk for the over-forty set. So busy trying to figure out their financial futures, they had no feel for fun. I wanted to scream we haven't gathered in this showy home to mourn, so why isn't anyone laughing without reserve until it spreads like sweet liquid down our lives? Our civil little lives!

Actually (as my husband likes to remind me several times a week, tops), I did yell that out. Rather loud and overconfidently, in fact. The very reason, for all concerned, why I was not invited back this calendar year.

THE TOY AISLE
December 2004

All it takes is a stroll through a convenience store toy aisle to realize what seed is being planted in the minds of our children: that warfare is commonplace, fun, an acceptable way to play on.

Presumably, the toy aisle I find myself in midway between men's Carthartts and the in-store post office is the boys' toy aisle. One perk of not having children is the luxury of avoiding such aisles; also why I probably sound pretty naive to parents familiar with toy arsenals. Yet, the visual assault astounds me. And the startling I feel is much bigger than my capacity for understanding why toy makers would want to promote plastic Repeater Rifles complete with "reliable rifle sounds" and "eject play bullets."

I read over this last paragraph and wonder if I'm the only one connecting the dots here, or is there something overly responsive, or too ridiculous about the way my mind interprets the world? Am I caring too much?

I know it takes a lifetime for boys to figure out what being a man is all about, but maybe, just maybe, if we didn't jump-start them with miniature F-5 Freedom Fighter Jets they wouldn't have lodged somewhere deep in their brains like the scent of Sunday pancakes the myth that fighting is some kind of fun.

Curiosity sparked, I check out the girls' toy aisle instead of leaving the store quickly as I'd entered. There is, to my mind, an even more scary mind set embodied in this aisle, and it's remarkable to walk through it, a way to understand our expectations for girls from an intimate perspective. Facing it, I feel sad; also resentful. Most prominent are baby dolls, blenders, toasters, and housekeeping sets, things June Cleaver does, I suppose, aproned and smiling, while boys are off driving Hot Wheels on the front lines.

Mind you, plenty of other toys are present: Legos, a slew of art supplies, puzzles, and board games. Even marbles. Wow, I think, marbles. Still, because action-for-boys and domesticity-for-girls remains the norm within the norm of mainstream toy sales, I question whether things have changed all that much since my mother's day. And all days prior to hers.

I know some of you are thinking that I'm hopelessly idealistic. But I think there's a better name for what I feel while staring at a 40-piece set of toy soldiers pointing guns at each other: off balance, the disquiet that comes from not understanding why things are the way they are, or why so much hollowness seems to fill the world. I guess I crave, the way others do sugar, some kind of proof that things will turn around. What wears away when I see weaponry-for-play is my hopefulness, every shard of it whittled down.

I'm not a religious person, per se. My way is not to defer joy until I reach heaven but to seek the ever-after in the here and now. And at the epicenter of my present is a hugely challenging creative life, a consciousness fueled by risk and hope. And only in its presence do I feel confident and capable. Without it I fear an overwhelming sense of unfairness will seep into everything I think, write, say, do. And I can't let that happen.

I figure I'll begin by avoiding toy aisles. Felicity, like any special set of circumstances, requires sound planning.

V.

"I like going to extremes. When people say,
'Don't go there,' I say, 'I'm going.'"

— Alfre Woodard

WHAT GOES AROUND
January 2005

For me, January is a month of selectivity. After a whirlwind of holiday socializing, gatherings where I'm too tightly held in to be myself, all I want is to bask in the safe company of good friends.

I mention this only because it points out something about making choices, which, when combined with the theme of "coping with winter," is a favorite subject of mine (I know you know). Because in January, no matter how long I live in this Northwest, I still have some, ahem, issues with the lack of sunshine. So, as gales gust through our seaport of a city, I seek from my friends the kind of laughter that spills in every direction. Accompanied by a white chocolate martini, the combination gives me a whole new perspective on wintertime.

Carving out one-on-one time with my inner circle of cohorts, women who strive to live fully and don't mind sharing what goes on with them, is my potion for contentment. These women don't wait, they risk. And no matter where we are in our lives, we share the details until some insight is ours, an exchange that uplifts the slump that sets itself down on me soon as the twinkling lights of holiday are gone.

Here's a story about one of these evenings that also posed a familiar challenge to women before it brought us back home to ourselves:

A friend and I walked under a full moon, one of those huge silent discs easy to blame for the heat rising in us. And for picking at our husbands with a fist of tension clenching our chests. There isn't one plight on being female that hasn't passed through us until we can find a so-this-is-what-our-mothers-meant pang of humor in it.

It was a perfect night to visit a local pub where beer is made in a metal vat steaming to heat those of us gathered at the bar. When I laid my hands on the cool, varnished wood, it warmed. In fact, the whole place warmed, enough to bathe in conversation, in a friend's dread of hormones if that's what she needed, in the scent of hops brewing behind us.

But for everything meaningful that the night *was*, it was not the night to make room for a tourist's string of questions—where to eat? what to see? where you from?—because I hadn't seen my friend in a while, too long to share her with a man we didn't know. We were deep in friendship, bordering on spiritual connection, which could not be explained to a guy in ten words or less. I cleared my throat more to end his queries than anything. No such luck. He pretended the sound had nothing to do with him.

Under different circumstances, I have more patience for this line of questioning. Particularly in summer. But in the throes of winter on a weeknight, I want to feel as though our city belongs to us. Not to someone who appeared out of nowhere to assume we'd not just filled a space but vacated one where a man should sit. And just so you know, while clothes might not maketh the man, an overbearing stale smell of cigarette smoke definitely unmakes him.

My first instinct was to kindly (and by "kindly" I mean with enough edge) ask him to leave. When it comes to this preemptive measure, spare me from being pointlessly polite. Then, as if swearing has something to do with manliness, he mumbled how fucking unfriendly we were. Of course he did. And we could see every little ripple of the blasphemy swishing between his ears. Which caused my friend and me to turn to each other, touch hands to form a singleness to our disgust, before she answered him breezily, "I could have told you *that*."

Okay, that's just one reason I love her so.

I figured by morning, two women lost in their own conversation would already be a memory to him, blurred by distance and fog.

And the privacy my friend and I shared was well worth the humbling to come, for what goes around surely comes around. I fully expect that on one of my travels, someone will interpret my enthusiasm as an intrusion and I'll be on the receiving end of utter embarrassment.

But I can live with that.

ASH WEDNESDAY

February 2005

I'm a kid again, sitting in a pew in a Roman Catholic church, a stage set of a holy place in every way. Marble statues of saints, stained glass windows, bitter-sweet incense permeating the air.

When an altar boy swings the incense too close to our pew, my father warns him to "knock it off" in the same voice he uses when I annoy him. On Sunday morning, after a night of poker-playing and Scotch & soda debate, my father is a night's sleep away from civil, not about to let us enjoy the fairy tale he says religion makes of life.

My mother tries to convince me otherwise. And that the ashes we're about to receive won't hurt. "They're nothing like the ashes from your father's cigarette," she says.

She delights in the idea of repentance, its possibility, tells me I won't feel a thing but awe. Unlike my father's agnosticism, her devoutness seeps into everything she is, and like many with no formal schooling, she believes anyone of hierarchy, especially priests, is infallible, obliging them without question.

After dabbing his thumb in ash, the priest marks my mother's forehead while saying the words: "Remember man that thou art dust and unto dust thou shalt return." There is much to fear in those words. She accepts the ash with a bow of her head. I kneel to accept my fate.

There, it's done. Ash is fixed to the center of my forehead. I can't see it but I know it's there. And then, impossible as it seems and just as my mother promised, my self-consciousness sort of breaks up. As if whatever I was afraid of before the ash, I stand tall now. My mother smiles, drawing me toward her like a tide.

This memory is personal and history is collective. So here is where I add that Ash Wednesday is the first day of Lent, the seventh Wednesday before Easter, and that ashes are placed on the forehead to remind that man is mortal and it is dust to which we will return. At least that's how it works in theory. The practice, originally a Roman Catholic observance, has made its way into the wider church and even into popular culture.

I might have strayed from the practices of formal religion, believing a creative life rather than scripture will save me from darkness. Still, I can't think of anyone, whatever he or she believes, who couldn't use a little reminder of how fleeting life is, of ash placed just so on the brow.

THE SECRET PURPOSE
January 2005

This evening, with my right arm looped through her left, I walk with my friend. The air is so cold we shiver. This is the bane of our existence: winter. Still, with our heads inclined toward the words we share, we stop and relish the sky, the sea aglow in the distance, all the terraces twinkling with lights— not because they are beautiful, but because each is a meticulous effort to make contemporary architecture feel comforting and familiar.

We stroll down Vine Street, window shop our way along First, circle back on Second, sneak a peek inside one of the new dance clubs before agreeing we don't feel hip enough to go in.

From any vantage point, at any given time a city is so many things at once. Especially its core, where glass and chrome share the stage with crumbling brick. On Third Avenue I look into the eyes of a homeless man and I see the layers of resent- ment palpable as the sidewalk beneath him. I hand him five bucks and we walk up to Fifth, where the monorail sweeps over us, quickly gone as it had come. In a few short blocks I run the emotional gamut from elated to guilty. But it's my job, isn't it, to get along with all parts of myself?

No question, walks release me from the cloistered living inside of my head. Gut honesty mixed with laughter lightens my mood, oh, at least a ton as my friend and I clutch at ways to console. Firm as trees, we brace ourselves against the wind, convince ourselves we are not whining, then snuggle into Adirondack chairs chained to the roof of my condo.

It seems so obvious, but it takes us all night to figure out and affirm our brainstorm: that fear of something is not preparation *for* it. After that, we discuss the legitimacy of full spectrum light, the merits of vitamin D. Wonder at what age we'll seek a desert home to flee to in winter until, like the flocks of snowbirds before us, we stay through spring. And finally, each season back to back. I say by then my ass will have already traveled down south that far, and we laugh as hard from our mouths as we cry from our eyes. In the language of emotion, we are polyglots.

We need room to consider all this. And alcohol. We head off to find the best Dirty Martini in the neighborhood.

Ah. A few sips and I come full circle. Sharing a cocktail, like most intimacies, calls for a certain self-forgetfulness. And to my credit, it doesn't take me too many swigs to sense that the hidden truth of winter is clearly about friendship, the threads I tie myself together with. Decades deep into our familiarity, our plights, suddenly means more than any yearning for clear skies. This realization is a big red splash on my dull self-pity.

Because even on the shortest, darkest day of the year, light *is* shed between us, specific light that extends outward like the spokes of a wheel and yet still holds tight to the middle. All of which might sound a bit corny when referring to women but, in this case, the middle is *us*.

Which brings me, finally, to the secret purpose of winter: It's the season that asks us to need each other more than before. There isn't much more to it than that, is there? Sometimes a martini is not so much a drink as a salve, the cure it takes to understand. Sunshine pales compared to this change of heart.

Boy, that's hard to say. But as I consider the alternative, another slump stretched to the breaking point, it sounds heavenly.

DAUGHTER OF
ROMAN CATHOLICS
April 2005

The passing of Pope John Paul II causes anyone who has ever been a part of the Roman Catholic faith to mull over his influence, even if for the last thirty years both he and the church have existed only in the far corners of her mind.

Born to parents of Italian descent, what choice did I have but to be raised Catholic? Before sleep I'd stare up at a crucifix until I found the courage to remove an anguished Jesus to make room for a smiling John, Paul, George, & Ringo. Braced with preteen will, I remember thinking no man nailed to a cross was going to dictate to me, probably the main reason my father clocked a fair amount of time sliding his belt backward through each loop while counting to ten.

Today his form of discipline sounds beastly. But to his credit, the fear he instilled in me was likely the only reason I was never in any serious trouble, too scared of the consequences at home to pop acid, shoplift, or lose my virginity. But, at fifteen, under a canopy of grapevines, I faced a fear more palpable than one of a God I couldn't see. Struggling against my father's anger equaling my own, I grabbed the strap from his hands. You can imagine how such a defiance went over.

A stubborn man and a headstrong girl make for two tempers in full dress. I remember running, halting, turning dead on to face him. How he stumbled breathless, the smoker he was. How fear filled me with will and when I swung the belt, the world was suddenly terrifying and yet safely my own at once. And as he walked away in silence, absolute confidence grabbed me under the arms and lifted. But the sureness was fleeting. When my feet found earth again, I felt inexplicably sad and afraid, audacity no match for teenage vulnerability.

That confrontation occurred because of the Pope, or rather because of something I'd said earlier about the Pope, one of those statements kids make in order to throw their weight around even if the load amounts to, say, 90 pounds of insecurity. "I don't care what any Pope says, I'm never getting married and I'm never having kids and I'll sleep with whoever I want!" Without the diplomacy to know how to prod my mother's awareness, I behaved as if I had a right to trounce it. (I still struggle with this.) She reacted with one of her looks, conveying disappointment with just her eyes. And then she did what she always resorted to when her faith met my rebelliousness. She yelled for my father. "Luigi!"

Like many who made it through a world war, my parents don't talk much about the hard realities of warfare, preferring to focus on the possibilities ahead. Though the Vietnam War raged for most of my youth, our home sort of sleepwalked through all of that. I can't remember one engaging conversation about Vietnam or the changing social fabric all around us. At the dinner table, we watched the evening news, updated nightly with a body count, yet no discussion of war ensued, no mention of what it was like to nearly starve to death (my father did) under Mussolini's rule.

My father spoke of war's hardships only with my aunts and uncles who'd also escaped a devastated Italy. Wanting to spare his children, he never discussed his war-torn past with my sisters and me.

But instead of feeling spared, we felt outside of him as he forged his way into middle American society with a vengeance. As a good Catholic he fathered three children in six years, a number that would have doubled or even tripled had my mother not suffered complications that dictated I was to be her last child.

As for my mother's say in child rearing? She would not have disobeyed a Pope who, much like her father, her husband, her priest, pretty much dictated her choices so that she still finds it difficult to make a decision without a man's say-so; longing, I suppose, for the days when men were men and women were, other than in domestic roles, unaccountable. A seed of independence never took root in my mother's consciousness. Which couldn't be more unlike the experience of her daughters raised on American soil. In the 70s!

To this day, my mother and I can't discuss the Pope without a verbal head-banging. Last try, I didn't help any by saying that every Pope looks pretty much the same to me: an out-of-touch white guy in medieval robes. A man I stopped paying attention to not purposely. Or consciously. The desertion seemed more natural than something decided. More like spontaneously in response to the fact that none of the church's leaders were of my gender, other than Mary, who supposedly gave birth while still a virgin. Right.

At the same time, I liked Pope John Paul II. Knowing he condemned abortion for the same reason he denounced capital punishment, believing human life should never be destroyed intentionally, made it easier for me to identify with him. Unlike moralists who oppose a woman's right to choose under the same pretense and then, in the next breath, wage war.

So as I muster up the courage to call my mother to discuss the passing of John Paul II, I warn myself not to disregard any of its effect on her, nor the church's for she hates that I've left it, that I mistrust its doctrine, that I live in a city she's never seen leading a life she calls spiritually *iffy*.

But then, I'd have to agree with her there. Some days I am entirely sure of what I believe in terms of a divine path. Yet most days, holy cow, I don't have a clue.

WHY HAVEN'T WE

March 2005

I wonder if violence is the surest and, in some cultures, the only way left for a man to define himself as male?

This is the question that forged through me as I stood in a Costa Rican jungle where prolonged guttural ululations between two male Howler monkeys both awed and depressed me. Chin back until I couldn't stand any longer, I sat on the jungle floor with my knees drawn to my chest as if to keep my reverence even closer. And for weeks now, I've been unable to turn any of what I felt into words. I think fear kept me from trying.

War is often described in ways that suggest it's unique to people. But one listen to two male Howlers defend their turf of Jacaranda, and the reality that the world is not peaceful is blatant, even if you have no difficulty imagining it so. Sitting there in a flow of insects, I sensed how the male species is biologically programmed to check out the nearest competition and act aggressively in order to preserve itself.

I don't know what anyone else would have done at such a time. I suppose some would look up, smile, and keep walking. I know a Costa Rican would, after giving me that "poor thing" look because I was solita (alone) in the woods without a man.

156

Unabashed curiosity undoubtedly defined me as "tourist." A good thing to remember the next time I hear a shriek of delight when a traveler to the Northwest spots a deer.

In 1948 Costa Rica abolished the army to save resources for its people. To compensate, the police force is heavily armed. Even security guards pack automatic weapons. I'm sorry, but this didn't instill in me a feeling of peacefulness. And it's why I left town to enter the jungle, where no man, left to his own limbs, is mighty. I went in to disengage, to listen from within.

Midday in Central America is relentlessly hot and bright, wearing every species down to a slothful pace. It's as if the whole continent is hibernating; everything about it slows. But the jungle is shaded and cool. And powerful. It reminds us that so much happens beneath the surface of stillness, making us more conscious of what lies within ourselves, of how silence serves both to stir up and settle.

And the jungle is where my nonviolent hopes for the world met real life—the reality, when beginning to write this, I was afraid to confront. Any wilderness offers this kind of naked truth. Perhaps the strongest argument to save our woods is to remind us the world has a plan for us no matter what.

But wait! Humans have the foresight to change the course of things in the same way we have altered the flow of lakes and rivers because, unlike other species, we can conceive of the future and build a better way. Right?

So my next question is, why haven't we?

Must I now acknowledge something even bleaker, that at a deeper level, we are still as primitive as the Howlers?

CREATIVE POSSIBILITY

April 2005

Ever since the spring of 2000, when millennium hype joined my realization that television is the greatest betrayal of intelligence, it's been my practice to unplug mine right about now when April sets in exquisitely green. And it remains unplugged until, say, late fall when darkness returns; nothing getting me through a Northwest winter better than flannel pj's, a good video, and yes, a little mindless relief *from* my intelligence. Such as it is.

My friend Rachel, an excellent mother and genuinely kind soul, has gone a step further. While my TV remains firmly in sight, she stows hers in the garage, explaining over the protests of her four-year-old son that she'd rather watch him for entertainment. This after he said he needed to have his teeth whitened so he could own (own!) a winning smile.

Well into the third or fourth day, after my self-imposed "no TV" rule is in order, I begin to sense a shift. And it's strong enough to readjust my outlook, a decompression that moves with relief into my limbs. Maybe it's just boredom shedding, I don't know, but in this state it's difficult to settle for something narrow as a network trying to undermine the self-trust that struggles to be free in spite of advertising that needs to sell me things.

Because do I notice how the ads targeted at women are nothing but a three-word message: *you need fixing?* I do. And if we watch long enough, the messages accumulate and are stored in our subconscious until any sense of creative possibility diminishes. If we conform to an image set by advertisers, their power is fixed. And it's why there is so little originality out there, why so many dress the same and think the same. For whatever reason, people begin to consider themselves original for opting for a product everyone else is choosing. Shopper meet corporate intention.

Yet even I, the nix-the-television advocate, have to double-dare myself to pull the plug because I know how much I'll miss *Will & Grace*, their fabulously uncensored humor, the Emmy-winning series that proved in the aftermath of the "Ellen" collapse that a story centered on gay characters can catch on with a mass audience and receive some of the highest ratings ever.

I point this out not because I hypocritically want to advocate a slice of TV viewing simply because it makes me laugh out loud (but you and I know that's precisely what I *am* doing because, out of nowhere, this paragraph opposes everything else I've said). And even if I didn't intend to head in this direction, I couldn't miss the opportunity, especially in light of certain right-wing agendas, to plant such a good seed of gay history.

Because after I've spent the day writing about past realities or future worries, I delight in any story that sets my mind squarely down on "right now" with a sense of humor mature enough to be true. It helps me appreciate everything good about the world. And that sometimes the best way, the only way, to the get to the truth of ourselves is to poke fun at our duplicities.

THAT SWEET SOUL MUSIC
May 2005

Anyone who's been a dancer since childhood and is dancing still, long after most of her peers have shed their dancing shoes to resettle into age-appropriate yoga, tai-chi, or water aerobics, will eventually face the question, "Are you still dancing?" Emphasis on the word *still*. Its long arm of implication reaching 'round.

And you know how hard it is to answer the question because at forty-something when each day is a swinging pendulum between young and old, there's so much to think about behind the feelings such a question arouses, the mix that has you staring out the window at 3 a.m. Usually I answer cheerfully, because I do, in fact, love my work as a dancer and choreographer. But sometimes the question provokes, and at that moment I try to remember the expression that there's a space between the brain and the mouth for a reason. That way I won't regress in an instant, saying something that struggles to sound at ease.

It's not that the question isn't well-founded. Most adults *do* move on from the strenuous workout and time commitment dancing involves, the kind of flexibility and cardiovascular stamina it takes to dance well. And one can't argue that physical ability does decrease with age. But not to the degree most assume. More accurately what happens is that life intervenes, and in our culture it's likely to be a sedentary one. When I think back on all it has taken to maintain fitness (no one in my family is naturally svelte), I can honestly say the main reason I continue to dance is simply because I can. And while I might have danced with more power when younger, that pales compared to how it feels to dance with the kind of resilience and tolerance-for-fear acquired only with time. Give this up for the taut tummy and mile-high leaps I once had? No way.

Lately, though, when I try to paint a mental picture of The Future, I think about what's in store, physically, when I finally take leave of daily dance practice. So I've packed up my work-out bag and gotten out there to try a few stretch-to-the-music classes, a dance-with-abandon-but-no-technique class (that seemed more like a social gathering), and a spin class that nearly killed me: What felt like eons later, I was finally able to breathe again, teaching me only that aging comes with many small affronts to one's dignity. And that humiliation is solid.

Because, ten minutes into each class, no matter how challenged I feel, I grow restless. For one thing, I long for the artistry that is not a part of such straightforward calorie loss, not to mention how out of place I am, a doubter in the church of health clubs, an agnostic in the New Age. Aside from the fact I want to run howling from people who use words like "free-flowing muscular energy," I end up quitting mostly because my boredom overrides any vigor, physical or otherwise. Add to the equation a low small-talk threshold and resistance to why any woman would mount a sports-logo over the tender flesh of her left breast and you've got a most reluctant student. Then there's the matter of all that hi-tech spandex. Is part of the workout squeezing into the outfit? Spandex. Even the word irritates me.

It's taken the last decade to realize how time urges me to be honest. And honesty is a way more generous thing than I could have imagined when I still feared aging so. Because, as beautiful as youth is, it is full of the kind of judgment people hold on to because they are not quite sure if they are A, B, or C enough, a world to outgrow. Somewhere, there must be a survey confirming that a very, very small percentage of the dancing population will continue to dance unashamedly, no matter how young and sleek the majority of dancers are, because with age comes giving a big fat shrug to what others think. When I look at the women and men who dance into midlife and older, whether in my class or someone else's, I think what a comfort it is to have us around.

Still, I've been close to quitting many times. Especially in those disconcerting moments when I realize I can't jump as high or bend as low, or when class goes badly or, worse, a performance. Anyone who thinks dying is the worst that can happen doesn't know a thing about live performing. How you can work and work and work at something and then suddenly, poof, it's over with so little memory of anything other than what went wrong.

And yet I'd be nowhere without my performance blunders. They've nudged me to face a medley of fears. Keep smiling, I say to myself when I misstep, and they'll never know I want to perish.

It would be easy to say I'll always dance, but it wouldn't be true. Every dancer knows this layer of intense conditioning eventually needs to shed itself. As much as I look forward to rewarding myself with a little less discipline, I'll always be grateful I resisted settling for a safe norm, that I pursued the passion that first seized me as a child when life stretched in front of me endless and free. And I like knowing how it feels to come to the studio without aspiration, competitiveness (with others or myself), or any of the other emotions that can haunt a younger mind and keep one from fully enjoying what it is we do. It's taken a lot of failures and a willingness to experience each to free me of anything other than pure love of the discipline.

Remember the song, *Do you like good music, yeah, yeah, that sweet soul music, yeah, yeah?* Most of my life I've sung these lyrics whenever things go awry, as if the words are written into my DNA. The song might be an oldie, but the bliss I feel when I dance to it is pure and never, ever outdated. It doesn't matter if I hear the song in a grocery store or a coffee line, I'm going to dance to it until, like the moment your ears pop, everything is even again.

VOILA! PARIS AGAIN

June 2005

After learning that I had accumulated enough mileage credits to fly to virtually any destination imaginable, it took me only a few seconds to say aloud the word, *Paris*.

Years ago, I'd visited the city as did so many hippie kids, with a backpack and a hundred bucks that needed to last me. It wasn't the right time to experience a city as culturally alive as Paris. Yet its contrast to American aesthetic, how it felt to weave through the remains of an ancient civilization, poured into my psyche and took root, lodged in me ever since.

On the way to the airport, just the thought of sitting in a wicker bistro chair while sipping white wine with lunch, red wine with dinner, or pink vin in between was enough to transport me, and as my taxi sped by Boeing Field, my gaze fell over the skyline until the rise of airplane hangars became the hills of Montmartre, Harbor Island the Left Bank of the Seine and voila!, Paris was alive in me again.

I think of Paris as my alter-ego city. Its maze of boulevards crowded with mini-cars couldn't be more unlike my newly sprung Seattle neighborhood, SUVs nearly the size of my studio condo wedged in along its streets. But any one of my friends would tell you another reason I love Paris is because I'm a shoe aficionado, heels specifically. The combination of my five-feet-two-ness and that I'm Italian makes my encyclopedic knowledge of shoes as natural to my small-talk as the subject of weather. Still, I had my concerns before traveling to Paris, the fashion mecca, that too many years in Seattle might have anaesthetized my ability to click along confidently in two pointy high heels. Because no way was I going to be one of those Americans in tennis shoes.

But what I found in Paris was that the women are not overly fashion-conscious. French women have far less disposable income then Americans. But they are noticeably at ease presenting themselves with flair and femininity. Paradoxically, fashion doesn't dictate in the fashion capital. Creativity, however, does. Why, I wonder, have so many American women settled for the athletic shoe, jeans, and sweatshirt habit? Do they realize, in terms of the art of dressing, how bored they have become?

Fortunately for me, as soon as my airplane touched down, my feet belonged. Luckily, I thought, the natives are friendly! And while some travelers recall the names of restaurants with pride, the loft of my memory is filled with the images of village shops on narrow, winding streets where my gaze fixed on a pair of leather shoes glowing like luminous gems.

"Pointy" comes and goes in American shoe aesthetic but is staple to the European sense of style. I'm forever telling people who stare with tortured eyes at my feet that no, I do not squeeze my toes into the point; the point extends *past* my toes. And I've taken a fair share of verbal flak for the Euro-pointies I prefer in a city that's all about an outdoorsy-fleecy look for both sexes all the time. In fact, recently as I stood on a sidewalk chit-chatting with a friend, a woman walked by, stopped, looked down, pointed at my shoes and said, "Why are you wearing *those*? reminding me that even in our most liberal of cities, shoe tolerance, in the minds of some, is moot. I sighed ... *Birkenstockies*.

France is situated between two major shoe-exporting countries, Italy and Spain. So it's not unusual to see shoes displayed like high art (actually they are high art, not a subject I wish to defend) on pedestals, lighting cast just so. I limited myself to four pairs because I always travel in the make-do-with-one-carry-on mode, which is sometimes easy, a lot of the time dismaying, but always necessary to my peace of mind.

Here is my pick of perfect vacation shoe memories that I will call: Perfect Vacation Shoe Memories:

Strappy-black heels from Paris. Every intimate desire of mine is gathered en masse in these heels, and when the day comes I can no longer manage to walk in them, they will continue to shine like their own bright star from a shelf in my closet.

Butter-soft boots from Provence. When first the shop owner could not find my size, I would not accept the misfortune and demanded he look again. (I am American, after all.) It worked, by the way.

Handmade in Spain shoes-soft-as-gloves from Cassis by the sea.

A pair of Italian slip-on sandals from Nice, ankle straps tough but not hard.

Whatever the explanation for a woman's fancy for shoes, perhaps the fact that in France it is illegal to work more than 35 hours a week and that each worker is given six weeks annual vacation time lends itself to a healthier balance in life. This fine sense of equilibrium, and how to maintain it, is considered vital to political platforms. Which might be why French women have time to consider themselves in the mirror and are comfortable walking in heels over cobblestone at a pace unhurried as they accept the time it takes to stroll properly, no connection to a culture (ours) that prefers every inch of time filled to the max while wearing clothes that are tediously comfy.

Just before I left the city, I stopped to listen to an accordion player fill the air with music. On his feet, a pair of black leather dress shoes, decades old, polished for performance. So, along with the change in my pockets, I threw him the kind of kiss where you scrunch your fingers together at your lips and release in an exaggerated gesture, letting your hand spread wide as you brandish your show of gratitude before yelling, *Bravo!*

And back home, I will continue to wear my heels that step with pride over the looks they draw, and kick away even the slightest possibility of settling for shoes that belong, to my eye, only on the basketball court.

THE INTRUDER

June 2005

There are a few things one can safely assume about life in small-town Northwest, in this instance, Port Townsend, Washington: When you grocery shop, you'll likely run into someone you know. If a corporate entity wants in, there's going to be a petition. Come fall, grass turns green again.

Not to presume, however, that your house can remain unlocked. Even if you're tucked away inside it working on your computer. And even if you can't bear to hear such a thing in your current perfect-Port Townsend frame of mind.

Nothing scares a woman more than the thought of an intruder. Worst-case scenario: Man sneaks in while she is asleep. But what if she is working in her office, listening to familiar sounds her husband makes walking in, midday, for lunch? But wait ... the noise is a little foreign, more labored than normal.

Admittedly, this is what happened to me. And my naivete scarcely exists since that day.

My cottage, located uptown, is in a "safe" neighborhood, right? Comparably speaking, this is surely true. Still, over the last decade I've had four bikes stolen, repeated smash-and-grab car burglaries, a horrifying experience with a peeping Tom. And once, in the time it took me to walk downtown and back (yes, leaving doors unlocked), all of my clothes were stolen, right down to the hangers and wooden dowel they hung from.

Still, these violations don't compare to the way it feels to find a strange man staring back at you in your own kitchen, causing me to take one, maybe two steps backward before bolting out the back door. And ever since, the thought that keeps haunting me is, "What if there had been no back door?" An image I don't wish ever to pursue.

I ran with a limitless sense of speed, acceleration I didn't know my legs could manage, to my neighbor's home, where Lou, an 85-year-old hero in my eyes, marched like a warrior over to my house to chase the trespasser from my yard, a confrontation that was a clash of opposite air masses so intense it might have spun a storm over the block.

After calling 911, police arrived in what I call " a New York minute" (yes, I thought, it's good to live so near a police station) to surround the intruder who was, I was later told, high from a spree of "gas-sniffing." Apparently he'd been sighted in other back yards around the neighborhood. Why, I wondered, had they not rounded him up before he found his desperate way into my home?

Why, indeed. We talk a lot about lifestyle in Port Townsend. But as good as it is for some, we are in the midst of what the victim/witness advocate told me is a meth-addict crisis spreading far and wide throughout our county and country. No matter what we'd like to believe, this is a problem that cannot be left behind when you pack up the moving van and exit the city for the idyllic small-town dream.

I have only column space, so I won't wade into financial politics, the utter lack of money to prosecute or rehabilitate addicts. Or how scary it was to learn this intruder already had a record in Port Angeles. So what did that county's deputies do with him? Well, according to one officer, they drove him out of their city which landed him, homeless, into ours.

We don't live in the kind of tight-fisted community where the disheveled, disoriented man who stumbled into my kitchen triggers a surplus of mistrust. Which in most instances, is a good thing. I don't want to live where suspicion breeds until there is a dull, suburban sameness to the look of things all around. Having said that, I will pay closer attention and won't hesitate to get involved if my gut goes aflutter for no reason other than one I'd rather deny. A neighborhood watch is not prying (as I once thought) but a responsibility.

And if I revert to routine as a coping mechanism by not locking my doors, because I want to believe I live one kind of reality while the facts of my life tell me different, this would be another sort of fearsome occurrence appropriately named "denial."

SERGEANT LEIGH ANN HESTER

June 2005

Whether or not women are strong enough to serve in the military has never been in question in my mind. Unless your argument is that in most instances, women aren't as physically strong as men of the same weight and stature, in which case I'd agree with you. Who wouldn't in the face of physiology? But this is not the kind of strength my argument leans on, even if almost no one seems to agree with me.

It's taken me awhile to enlarge on why I'm way up there in the ranks of those who propose women serving in the military, though God knows, I've tried to be sensitive to both sides of the issue. I've asked myself over and over why I hold to such an unfeminist view on this matter.

And today, as I await a flight out of Sea-Tac Airport, I ask myself again. All because an unlikely combination of one man I don't want to listen to and two televisions I don't want to watch has caused the question to resurface. And it's not a question of feminine nature as I first thought, but of human, with particular relevance for Americans at this time.

Confined in an airport terminal, it's surprising how much you learn about others. Enough to learn if you'd care to know them any further. Obviously, the man I don't want to hear is distraught. Also pushy and overbearing, and it's beyond me why he takes all this out on the ticket attendant. Perhaps someone can be outrageously rude to a counter attendant and in other respects considerate, but I doubt it. We are as we behave. I can easily picture him stealing my seat if I get up to throw my trash in the bin.

It's also beyond me why airports broadcast CNN just before passengers submit to a liftoff. Whenever people ask if I'm afraid to travel alone, my pat answer is "only of watching CNN at the gate." Its effect on me? A slow onset of fear because I'm easily mesmerized by the monitor, by the scary pace in which the images are delivered. And this is how I learn that Sergeant Leigh Ann Hester of the 617th Military Police Company (company? military police for profit?) has earned a Silver Star for Valor in Iraq, the first time the honor has been awarded to an American woman since World War II.

Mr. Airport Inconsiderate reacts to the news of Sergeant Leigh Ann with, wonder of wonders, indignation before informing the rest of us that "women for crying out loud don't belong in the military." Sometimes I think this war is blurring everyone's intelligence.

The thing is, I agree with him. Not with his reasons but in a different way. He made me think more about Leigh Ann. How when she is elderly and thinking back I don't think she'll be able to view killing three insurgents (whatever that means by now) point blank with a rifle as anything close to a shining moment in her life, no matter what horrifying struggle called for "taking them out." And in that sense, I'm grateful to this man, to what feelings about Leigh Ann he evokes, to giving me the chance to explore my feelings about this issue more deeply. When I think about it, the answer I've finally come up with isn't nearly as confusing as it sounds. To me, anyway:

Women are fundamentally different from men. Look how differently we view sex? No one argues that. I don't buy that a woman can kill another human and suffer it in the same way a man will, though both will suffer it equally. Clearly women have every capability needed in combat, but more to the point, I believe we serve mankind better by opposing war. And by doing so, we confront the horrendous-ness of choosing warfare as an option in a modern world, an alternative that makes nothing better for people other than those who profit financially, which is too weird and selfish to consider in relation to betterment *ever*.

For when have women not had to set the example of how to behave, how to turn inward for strength, especially when the world needs one set so badly? And by tuning inward I don't mean tightening the grip, but figuring out how to put something in front of you rather than trying to solve a problem by repeating a routine set behind. It's startling how much we learn and relearn, and forget, or choose to forget, over time. And we ignore what history has shown us, as if we are in the middle of a present with no connection to the past. I have burned both ends of this pitiful reality right to the center. And here is where I find Sergeant Leigh Ann.

And because this war is so ludicrous, I feel sad for her. Sad because I think justifying her actions later in life will be her greatest battle. Our tolerance for unjustness is fragile. It wears out. And where will that leave Sergeant Leigh and all the soldiers like her who have killed or died because a thinly veiled lie was told and its telling was to become their fate?

VI.

"The human spark of communication. But not for too long. Because good communication is stimulating as black coffee, and just as hard to sleep after."

— Anne Morrow Lindbergh

SAUDADES
July 2005

Some people live somewhere because family does. Others, because family does not.

I'm afraid I fall into the second category, living amongst friends, my attachments formed deliberately. And what happens over time to those like me is that friends become more like family than family.

I chose Port Townsend because, after growing up on the crowed, highly competitive East Coast, it seemed the best the world had to offer: clean air, picturesque-ness, open minds, and unlike any coastal city back home, a house I could afford. Mind you, this was twenty years ago. The first time I saw Puget Sound, the evening sun coloring its sky, I thought, "Another life is behind me now and I'm finally home."

That's why it's difficult to put a name to what I feel as of late, something blurred in the center of me. It's not intentional but it's not unconscious either. It circles around in the back of my mind. Routine flows around it.

It's as if I'm in-between, well, not homes exactly, but home-imaginings. Some might call it nostalgia. Others, a yearning.

All I know is that, without a clue as to what the sentiment is, I sit at my desk trying to describe to the unafflicted how it feels to have a sort of homing impairment.

The Portugese have a word for it: Saudades: A sense of memory for something that might not even exist; still, you long for it all the same. Oh great, I thought, knowing how I can agonize over things inferred or perceived but, still, hurt so bad.

I envy those rooted in the Northwest, who don't seem to go into shock, as I do, when fall creeps in around mid-August, who don't get peeved when one gray day of winter folds into the next. In their company I feel I live here, yes, but I am not *of* here. And when I recently read that "home becomes a place you come to hate as much as you love," how I resisted the words, unwilling to apply them to me. But we can't choose our feelings can we? We can hide them (though I'm not too good at that) but not select.

Part of the answer, I think, is a reason other than my background, aside from my sun cravings, and irrespective of my restlessness: I am a product of a free and privileged society blessed with a dizzying array of choices. The downside of this blessing? That there is always some new elusive possibility, ever enticing, right around the bend. And that my imagination tends to stretch beyond measure, outpacing the reality of where I am with the possibilities of where I could *be*.

So it looks as though I might be faced with home-befuddlement for some time to come because it occurs to me this might be nothing other than one of life's many transitions forever taking me by surprise. That I simply need to brace myself, as if between waves, and hold steady.

And given a choice between an eternity or a temporary passage, I'll gratefully go with the latter because the chances of my packing up and moving on are growing less and less now that I've found a sense of familiarity in the world. Which is no small solace to a writer who wants, once her workday is done, to step out of herself and into comfortableness.

And even if this confused sense of belonging arises from time to time, well, it's just the way life breaks through sometimes, isn't it? Just so we can peek inside.

UNCLE PETE
May 2005

A couple of days ago, I came across a deckle-edged, sepia-toned photo, the kind of print that instantly reminds how fleeting time is. In it, my Uncle Pete squats in his beloved vegetable garden in rural Connecticut, where most of my family migrated after leaving the city behind. Five feet tall and nearly as wide, my uncle bore a smile that made him seem playful, if a little scary, to a young girl used to the long-standing misery of other "old-world" relatives too full of loss to lighten up, aunts and uncles who'd escaped Italy and immigrated to America, obliging the next generation to suffer the World War experience, word-for-word, so that whenever I heard them coming, I'd draw back and hide.

A contemporary writer might describe Uncle Pete as in-the-now or in-the-know, or candidly European, displaying the kind of enthusiastic behavior often looked down upon in polite American society. He'd talk with his hands and belly laugh, convey head-on honesty instead of niceties. But what I loved most about him was his unique way of making others feel as comfortable in his presence as he was with himself. He was my first example of an unorthodox man, for he led a daring life others only dream of. Not a life others tried to make him live or the kind convention celebrates, considering he had no money to speak of. What he did possess was an enviable way of being on his own side. A generous partner to himself, he had, to my mind, a relationship that far exceeds marriage, parenthood, and friendship combined.

Funny how I sat down to write about basil, its intoxicating fragrance so potent I can follow it through any market because more than I love the smell of basil, I love eating it. Yet, what I have is a description of my favorite uncle because, as any writer can tell you, this is how the process unwinds. It's not my conscious mind that dictates, but a voice that lives way deep, surfacing only when I tune in and listen hard.

And I am convinced I learned how to "tune in" in Uncle Pete's garden. I wasn't allowed to help, but believe me on this, anyone watching him work was immediately *involved*. By witnessing his love for tomatoes, peppers, and his favorite herb, basil, I became a gardener-by-osmosis. I didn't long for vegetables, but the ease I saw in his eyes, an expression I didn't see in the eyes of my friends or family. Inspired by the idea of concentrating on an effort until it gave me back an absolute sense of myself, he was my vehicle into a confident world, which was eons more desirable than the one I mostly lived in back then: a peer-pressured world, where fear and a need for acceptance (masked as confidence) make kids do some really selfish things.

Having referred to my uncle again, I realize this story will never be about basil—other than the model of discipline gardening set down for the rest of my life—but about a man who looked inward and showed me how to do the same, which has pretty much been the aim of my writing ever since: about finding an inner strength in the center of a busy life, more about a writer than a gardener. And certainly more about a man than an herb, but whatever it is, my thoughts have settled down and that's all I ask when I focus first thing in the morning, trying to make something whole in order to put it behind me.

A WRITER'S TRIBUTE TO FALL

September 2005

In my world, the single hardest day of the year is the one when I realize my container garden has dwindled to one hollow-eyed daisy on a gangly stem, drawing an imminent division between summer and fall in my mind if not on my balcony. Ever since June, July possibly, I did not resonate much to things beyond the warm day at hand. No sir, autumn had nothing to do with me.

And that's why every year around this time, as September fades full-tilt into fall, I need to repeat this affirmation: I can cope with the months to come, I can, I can, I *can*. Saying so reminds me that the most common and dangerous hunger in humans is the desire to control. Because when I step outside to inhale that first whiff of cold, I am thrown into a state of *wanting to* control. At least the weather. Or the role it will play in my life. But what I crave is to be at peace with it.

So as I go about garnering a slew of sling-back sandals bought for my alter ego who lives, unabashedly, in the tropics, I begin the process of balancing the sun-lover inside me with appreciation of the climate I make my home in. Until I feel rather fond of the gray skies and rain. Well, not fond exactly. But lighter for some reason. Which, in turn, moves me closer to appreciation rather than resentment.

My conscience, however, is not so convinced. A suave devil's advocate, she has seen my silk skirts and spaghetti-strapped camisoles. Not to mention my ease on a bicycle. And though well-intentioned is not a hyphenated word I like to call myself, she knows that's my leaning. "Maria Louisa!" she scolds with the whole of my inherited name, sending me into immediate submission. Then she shrugs. I hate that: the shrug of all-knowing. Even when it winds straight to the truth.

I prefer to think that, comprised in her righteousness (that is really something more generous than that) is proof of her loyalty. Especially when it's summoned from a well-worn perch on my shoulder: "Listen!" she says. "More than half your body weight is H2O. Nothing gets past this fact of water, this way of things."

After a deep sigh, she continues with a self-satisfied smile wide enough to hold my past, present, and evolution in: "Sweetie, without rain we are that plywood fruit stand buckled over at the edge of suburbia, vanished along with any sign of its past. And girl, there is no difference between a fruit stand and you."

And since she is as relentless as someone else I know, me, and because I have no creed of my own to make sure my will is roused into place, I gratefully go with hers. Succumbing is easy, like pulling spuds from the ground.

Still, the day will come when I *must* face my intrinsic disposition. When even though I'm appreciating my green and leafy life, I whine about it more. The day desire overwhelms until all I can think, dream, muse about is my cold feet basined in warm sand. That and the fact that slow-spinning ceiling fans are suddenly my sole reason for living on this earth. The day I ask myself, anew, if I'm going to have to deal with this sun-dependency for the rest of my life?

Well, yes. Apparently so.

Which brings me to why I will spend the rest of the afternoon online until I find an affordable winter flight to the desert. Mexico. Hawaii. Any sunlit oasis, real or fabricated, will do so that upon my return to Sea-Tac, another question will arise: How many layers of fleece do I need to wear to retain the renewed sense of balance I've come home with?

And yet—and here's where the tribute comes in—I owe each and every work I've published to living in the Northwest. Nothing keeps me stationed at my desk like clouds growing dark as my eyes and hair. Because rain is the very tendon that binds me to my work, that replaces outside-ness, all the other things I do when the air is clear and warm.

What's invaluable to remember, for me anyway, is that for the past two decades, the Northwest has taken me seriously, or seriously *apart*, as I dig in toward the center of things a word at a time. The result of this connectedness? My life belongs to me in delightfully new and unexpected ways. Like a good friend, a sunless day gives me back to myself.

Bless the drizzle for that.

FOUR DAYS ON 89TH STREET
September 2005

Ah, yes, is what I think as soon as I step from my plane into LaGuardia to catch the announcement, "Would the passenger Tony Massiotti please report to baggage claim."

I hear the name the way others might revisit a birdsong. It puts me right back. I imagine Tony's slick black hair and a gold cross round his neck, his manner wrapped in a pelt of machismo, his mother living in the rowhouse next door.

Then there's the third world-ish feel to the airport: smaller, dingier, with stairs to reach baggage claim, no escalator. For a moment, I'm startled. Seconds later, recognition arrives: This is America's old country. How much newness, convenience, and space we grow used to on the West Coast, living between minute-and-a-half-old walls.

This dissimilarity between New York and Seattle, prompts me to call my husband to laugh about the man next to me who is not "fighting" with his wife and she is not "fighting" with him as they yell at each other contentiously. But any number of my Seattle friends would think they were about to commit a double homicide as they lapse into a loudness that intensifies under the slightest bit of stress. I call my husband because we've had to work on this, he and I, he from the laid-back-I-never-show-emotion-Scotch-Irish tradition, raised in San Francisco and, years later, finding himself married to an East Coast Italian girl impassioned easily about any old thing.

Besides, my people aren't from midtown or uptown, where the fashionable go-getters try to make it in a city that means they could make it anywhere. Italian immigrants settled downtown. And I don't mean The Village, as in East or West, but below Houston Street. Which any New Yorker will tell you "is a whole nudder thing."

Here's the good news: I've been lent the keys to my publisher's pad on the upper West Side, just a few blocks from Central Park. Which means to my family that "I've come up in the world." And I suppose it means the same to me. Still, on the sidewalk I identify with the Ecuadorian maids and nannies, rather than the chiseled, blond women of means (my cabbie still calls them "aristocrats") who seem so fearless and entitled. I look at them and know I will never be able to be so blase about privilege. It doesn't matter how many years have passed, how much wealth I've attained or success I've met, in this city I feel my proletarian roots resist, my past and present playing tug-of-war to and fro.

Among this jumble of emotions is the feeling that I might have a big ol' dose of homesickness. Not only for a city that lets me wear pointy heels without staring down as if I've just dropped my drawers, or for the buzz of it, which I actually prefer to, say, a walk in a national park, but for how people don't seem to want to keep the mess of the world at bay by moving to the suburbs and mowing compulsively. Instead they seem to embrace the street, accepting that it's impossible to hide from the harshness of the world.

And the doorman at my building on West 89th? He could be my cousin. He walks this block with such verve, such pride, such possession. God, I adore him. And when he hails me a cab by stepping right into the flow of oncoming traffic like a modern urban warrior, I think I'm in love. And because his mood is so down to earth and accepting of the caste system that plays itself out each day on this island metropolis, so, by association, becomes mine.

As a young person straight out of a girls' college (my father believed it would keep me unsullied ...), I was too intimidated by the "roar of the greasepaint, smell of the crowd" to compete. Maybe if my parents had been educated and not of immigrant status, I would have had a jump-start into a life of prestige that is the very ticket one needs. That is, of course, if I didn't want to end up north of 120th Street or south of Canal, living with five roommates in a stifling walk-up. Which isn't fun at any age and why so many young hopefuls end up in Queens.

And if I had been born to a different set of circumstances, would I have made it in this city? Why yes. No. Possibly. I don't know. Most likely. Who knows? All I know for sure is that right now, I'm swinging a bag of ridiculously expensive, exquisite groceries from Dean & Deluca's. And I can appreciate the blissfulness of doing so in a way I might not if this city had forced me to admit that my competitive edge is on a par with an eraser. At this moment the simplicity of a life free from such vigorous rivalry is mine, and before I return to Seattle, I'm pretty certain I will remember anew that some people are better off living in The Apple. But I'm not one of them.

I have no doubt that's the thought that will become clear in this out-of-reach city as I feel the relief of being here in an undemanding way.

Because on this particular sunny fall day, Manhattan belongs to me: from the food to the theaters to the fashion to the neighborhoods as distinctly different as men are from women. From the man on 96th Street whose yarmulke blows off in the wind, to the Jamaican nanny who runs after it. From the dog in Bryant Park who makes a living for his owner by balancing two smaller dogs, pyramid-style, on its back. To the nail salon on Columbus, where my feet are blissfully massaged even as cops ask the owners questions because only yesterday a wife was shot dead by her estranged husband right *here* (I swear I'm not making this up!). And yet, I'm ashamed to admit, I still enjoy my pedicure.

And from Little Italy, down around Elizabeth Street, now so hip that I fear my ancestors are revolving in their graves much like the rotisserie chicken they once sold here.

For me, this is as good as good gets in Manhattan. And there is no way I will spend another minute measuring my life against the choices I might have made. It will only rob me of the very thing I once thought an "uptown" life would bring.

Because, finally, here I am. One week. All mine.

RENEWAL
October 2005

On a warm evening last April, the new Aldrich's Market opened its doors and Port Townsend gathered to celebrate the rebirth of a store that serves as sort of a congregation for those of us with homes uptown, a core of community that even in its absence of one year and part of another, remained so.

How we've waited for time to reset itself, missing our daily walk to a neighborhood grocery, rather than driving, suburban-mode, to the mega-stores on the periphery of town.

The thing is, and this will sound strange, here it is fall and I still think about the huge gaping hole the fire left behind, the one now blessedly in the background of our memories. Somehow it's nonexistence feels like its own bereavement, whole as it began to seem, regardless of the void it made. A presence so intense it would affect me before I was fully aware of looking at it.

Only twice before have I stared into such an abyss so that my perspective forever changed. One was in New Mexico, where I stood on the rim of a silver mine, staring into a massive pit of emptied earth where, from my side of a chain-link fence, a man was explaining how silver is excavated. And I listened because I needed to hear what a miner saw in such an heinous site. For how could I object to mining's impact on environment when there I stood wearing my own curves of silver—bracelets, earrings and rings—like ornaments to my hypocrisy?

And when I stumbled away from the hollow in lower Manhattan where the western world's confidence came undone, I felt I might hobble forever.

But somehow neither of those experiences affected my psyche the way my first look into the wide-open nothingness off Lawrence Street did. In that space, I became wordless with personal loss, and though I turned away from the pit, I couldn't turn away from a vulnerability that seemed to slant through my days like rays of light. Only they were dark.

I came to think of that hole as its own detachment from troubled, worldly times, and whenever I peered into it, I too let go of something. Forced to witness how quickly the past can vanish, I could see how endless the possibilities are for restoration. The excavation began to speak in the same way a painting can. It altered my take on the world.

And so, a new store with bright orange awnings has sprung from the ashes, and I shop there faithfully not only to show gratitude but also because we share an intimate history of renewal. How many in our country in this day and age can say that about a grocery store?

I figure Aldrich's Market and I have a bond which like any relationship requires both parties make equal efforts.

THE RACCOON, MY HUSBAND, MY NEIGHBOR & THE HOUSING MARKET

October 2005

A few months ago, on a windless summer night, my husband and I woke to a frightening noise overhead. It sounded as if something was tearing a huge hole in our roof. Something was. A raccoon in desperate need of a warm and protected nest to bear her young, a raccoon that does not think of cedar as mine. And who could blame her? In her time of need, should she be expected to distinguish a level of shingles from the blunt side of a tree? What expectant female wouldn't do the same when faced with the alternative: having to claw her pregnant way into a vertical trunk.

We jumped up, scrambled into clothes, ran outside. But as I watched my husband assume a tentative posture while saying, "Hey, get down, shoo, hey you, shoo!" and throw the meanest weapon he could find, a *pebble*, all while wearing my bathrobe, I knew I had to call our neighbor. I needed old-fashioned manly know-how, a man born and raised in the house next door, a man with a pellet gun.

Like most of my neighbors, I've chased off many a raccoon. Also deer, coyote, squirrels, even a rat swinging trapeze-style from my bird feeder so that I had to stop feeding my flock of songbirds. Which led to a week of angry finches dive-bombing my window as if to say, "Hey! Aren't you forgetting something really big here?"

Still, aside from the day I came face to face with the deer who strolls around town with his tongue hanging out, this is the first time one of these backyard creatures became to me, well, shoot-able.

My neighbor appeared, gun cocked, forcing my husband to the woodshed to "get a ladder or something," not wanting to be seen, I suspect, in a knee-length robe, while I stood on the lawn jumping up and down, yelling swear words at the raccoon. She responded by tearing even bigger chunks off our roof.

Unflinching, my neighbor fired a shot at the raccoon. Not to kill her (because I told him if he did I'd have to kill *him*), but definitely close enough to force her off the roof, leaving a good part of it torn right through to the insulation.

Later, back in bed and dismayed, we peered out our skylight, trying to ease the looming cost of a new roof. But apparently the weight of another setback brewed even stronger: embarrassment. My husband couldn't reach past his to sleep. After tossing round, he finally let it spill: "You call yourself liberal? So what do you do soon as things get a little scary? You call a man with a gun!"

"A *pellet* gun." I reminded him, but really, is there any way to console a man with wounded pride? I *did* want the man next store to rescue us. Because even as it was happening, as my husband and I danced around trying to figure out a plan of action, I knew we were an inexperienced team of ex-city-ites, unequipped emotionally or practically to handle the beasts of the wild, wild west.

As much as it saddens me, Port Townsend is changing fast. People I don't know are everywhere, driving very expensive cars. And where does that leave my neighbor-with-pellet-gun? Well, he's selling his family house because, frankly, he can't afford to keep it. This makes me nervous, not only because I won't be able to rely on his know-how when a swarm of wasps invades the woodpile, or a coyote swaggers through my yard in open daylight looking for another cat to swallow. But because I know what his house is selling for. And I fear neighbors with that kind of dough will be worse than we at managing our backyard counter-attacks.

As pat as the saying is, it's true that nothing lasts forever. That for many years we could count on our neighbor to bring us slabs of salmon freshly caught and to have the proper shears for pruning made life better for us. And our new composite roof? Declaration to a man willing to leave his home in the middle of the night in order to make ours a little safer.

We probably won't have a sentimental send-off before he leaves, and most likely his dog will poop in our yard again, but I'm grateful he's been my neighbor. This is my way of saying good-bye.

THIEVES

October 2005

I've just finished performing *The Immigrant's Table* for two hundred people at The Market Theater in downtown Seattle, a topnotch, intimate venue tucked into one of the European-like cobblestone alleys that exist only in Seattle's Pike Place Market district.

The fact that I've managed to convince dozens of theater directors as well as writing conferences, universities, corporate and fund-raising boards that a staged reading of poetry can and will hold the attention of a theater-going audience is cause for celebration. But tonight I celebrate much more: Both the Bronx-born actress I work with and I "nailed it," a feeling that comes after you have practiced and practiced at something and just shown the world your best work. The high reminds you of how alive you really are. And it's fleeting.

Anyway, after the performance, I'm standing in the lobby signing copies of my book when a man approaches. Instinct tells me I'm not going to like what he has to say. Part of me wants to hop over the book table and run back stage to hide. So much for elation, I think.

Now it's just me and him. Or so it feels like. And this is what he, in my moment of celebration, chooses to say to me, "You need to speak from lower in your diaphragm. I've worked in theater, you see, and I think maybe ..."

After his first few words, my high fizzles. Oh I forgot, I mumble under my breath, this evening is really about *you* isn't it?

Those of us who perform know we must endure criticism. It's essential to our growth and is why a good director is vital to a show's success. But listening to sideline evaluators pointing out our every flaw directly after our performance is not a welcome part of the learning process. Instead, these unsolicited comments create a deep ache throughout the body of the actor (or dancer, or artist, or any brave soul willing to risk) at a time when relief is deserved.

"Tell me," the man continues, "do you have a degree in theater?" Oh, I just love this question. As if reading for the public for over twenty years is not an education. Academia is rich only in the size of its ego.

Let me ask you, do people walk up to a greengrocer to tell him his apples are stacked neatly but what about those messy bananas? Unlikely. Instead, we appreciate it's a difficult balance, all that wobbly fruit, with considerations we can't begin to comprehend. So why this need to level a performer's enthusiasm with the kind of appraisal so often earmarked for those working in the creative arts?

By now you might be thinking, "But the grocer doesn't invite an audience to view his work." I disagree. What if next time you shop, your fruit and veggies are thrown together willy nilly in a heap of mixed carbohydrates?

"Well," the man huffs as I turn away, "I thought I could help."

I've got news for him. In the real world, his kind of "help" is usually "control by manipulation."

For just what did he expect me to do with his advice now that the performance was already history? Because you know what? I know it's flawed. What work isn't? And I know my voice is sort of high-pitched. I'm working on that. What annoys me is that he thinks I can't realize the truth of my own imperfections without his informing me. To be reminded of what's missing and not congratulated for daring to try has only to do with his insecurity, not mine, even if that's not how it felt initially. Maybe, just maybe, this man hasn't put himself on the line in a very long while and faultfinding is his only effort in years.

Because in order to do the work a creative life demands, we have to refuse to accept a reality of limitations, to pursue inadvisable careers, to double-dare ourselves when we know there will be no reward other than the celebration this man nearly stole from me, a moment no one gets to stay in very long.

A WHOLE NEW ERA

November 2005

There are those who look back on Thanksgiving feasts with fondness and forward to Christmas with enthusiasm. But I am not one of those people.

Holidays were not easy around our house. My parents, divorced when I was a teenager, had a turbulent marriage long before they could untie the frayed strings of attachment that for years defined their marriage. What I remember is the simmering hostility in their eyes, like clouds passing in front of the glowing star children want the holidays to be. It felt like too much angst and letdown around our table. It overwhelmed me.

As time wore on, I learned the best way not to brood about my family life was to write about it, first in a lock-and-key diary where each night I'd clarify the details of my disappointments, digging in until I'd start to understand, amazed at the power of writing even then. Ever so slightly I would move from melancholy to a sense of pride. Which is still pretty much how the process unfolds for me today.

Fearing that my friend's families were better than mine or pretending that mine was better than it was didn't help. Regret surely didn't, and doesn't now, other than the level of conscience

197

it can call up, sometimes the very thing I need to balance the even longer thoughts that long to confiscate my sleep.

This is exactly how it happened for me one wakeful night when I got up, went to my computer and wrote my first e-mail to my mother. Why I couldn't sleep no longer matters, but what I found in the sleeplessness is the new story of my mother and me, champagne-able in terms of celebrating.

Because lately, whenever anything good happens, I assign great importance to it. It brings me into a brighter middle, overriding my peripheral fears. The same reason the poorest cultures in the world hold tight to their traditions. So they won't lose heart.

Which brings me, more directly than it might seem, to why this Thanksgiving marks a whole new "era" for my mother and me. Which is close to a miracle in status. By exchanging e-mails she and I finally found a way to share the truth of our family's dissolution as it unfurled in the past, which freed us to look at ourselves as we are now.

It wasn't easy. After threatening to store the computer her husband bought for her in the garage, which is her way of putting it down, she finally called that "nice young man" who works at Best Buy. He's part of a computer team called *The Geek Squad*, and my mother thinks it's because he's unmarried. I love the fact that a twenty-five-year-old guy is patient enough to sit with my 79-year-old mom until she learns to trust the memory "bank" she thought money could be deposited into (directly into) after he suggested she manage her checking account online.

To commemorate this new stage of our mother-daughter work-in-progress, our plan is to write each other every day. Now that we've learned not to come to our exchanges laden with bags of family history but only to pluck from the present, the tension between us is pretty much gone. This, only after we tried and failed to understand our past mistakes with frantic phone calls and countless self-examinings. None of which ever worked. So we decided that is exactly how important they needed to be.

At first we had to tug, push, and poke our way through old habits, hobbling two steps forward, tumbling back, neither willing to dilate, to open into the other's point of view. At one point I remember thinking that it's a miracle one of us hasn't pulled out the computer plug by now. Geeze, I thought, sanctimoniously, what is her *problem*?

But then a friend lost her mother, and then another friend lost hers, and guilt arrived. I felt a sudden need to move beyond our silly struggles. The hardest part was letting go of who I thought I was and seeing myself clearly through the magnifying lens of my mother's eyes. And not being afraid to remain there for the duration of our exchange. From there our patience seemed to go from withered to fertile in the span of a day. And I began to know her through words as I never could through long-distance conversation.

Her first e-mail said only: "Can you read this?" arriving six times because I suspect she approached the send button much as she does cooking: Why make a saucepan of soup when you can make enough to feed the neighbors, the bridge club, even the mailman?

This week, our e-mails naturally veer toward the one big thing we have in common: how to handle our frizzy Italian hair. "You have to get a really tight hat," she writes, "and pull it down over your head. A day of that, and your hair is smooth as a blonde's." Then she sums up our problem in a few, if unromantic, words, "Pull a nylon stocking over your head when you sleep." My mother pooh-poohs blow dryers with the same dismissal she once reserved for computers.

I'm not sure why we bemoan the fact that people don't write letters anymore. I think e-mails are better. Sometimes my mother's message is nothing but a matter-of-fact itinerary of her day, but like any good writing, facts alone are never enough. That's why I cherish her latest words, a tiny glimpse into a huge fear: "You know," she writes, "I've never really known what I want to be when I grow up." A bolt of connection shoots between us.

I don't think, pen to paper, this admission would have come. The task of finding paper, envelope and stamp might have forestalled the effort, the insight never shared. Strange, but the immediacy of e-mail has become the slow deliberation of us.

My mother and I live across the country from one another. Yet thanks to a technology I never plan on comprehending, I'm sure we'll run into each other again tomorrow, right over there by the in-box, on a screen that is the size of a thing that should not be able to hold so much.

TRAVELING HOPEFULLY

November 2005

As a Northwest woman, I thought I knew all there was to know about drizzly skies. Then I got older and, ahem, older still. Until I realized that in terms of my forty-something body there's nowhere to run to babeee, nowhere to hide. Now the rain not only affects my mood when all I want to do is cozy in with a hot toddy, it affects my bones. That's right, right down to the marrow, which is an entirely new way to experience my personal depth.

Lots of losses mount as we get older. And whenever I start to dwell on this scary truth, I stare at the maple tree outside my office window, a vast sprawl of leaves in summer, a dark mesh of leafless-ness in winter, with all degrees of growth in between. I'm told she's more than a hundred years old and just look at *her*. She's still got it going on, she's gorgeous! And when that ornery someone in the neighborhood complains about her falling leaves "messing up" the sidewalk, I shake my head, refusing to let his leaf anxiety effect my appreciation in any way.

A friend whose name will remain anonymous is a decade older than I and she is still so staggeringly beautiful and fit, though she won't believe a word of it ever. And yesterday she ventured to the mall. Why? Because when a woman wants a little pick-me-up, a bit of confidence (false? who cares!), or just a little guidance from her inner fashionista to hoist her femininity out of cold storage under the guise of "I need some new underwear," that's where she heads.

Maybe this wouldn't apply to the women who would never admit to shopping for fun as they walk around in $150 vests from R.E.I. As if purchasing something in an outdoor boutique is not the same thing *at all*. The thing about this kind of shopper is: She lies.

Anyway, back to my friend who found herself in the ultra-trendy FOREVER 21 store, where clothes are cheap enough to buy something really adventuresome to wear once, maybe twice, before it gives way. Still, it's the one store that had the sweater she'd been searching for. "It's just that when I got to the counter," she confided, "I felt the need to tell the little girl who waited on me that the sweater was for my granddaughter!"

Then, after admitting she ran to her car hugging the fluorescent yellow bag with its huge FOREVER 21 logo to her chest as if she'd just bought porn, we laughed to the point where you just know you're going to pee your panties, and I remember why I love her so much. Our honesty is the most phenomenal empowerment.

Because of her, and of course, my deep-rooted maple tree, I enter this whole new phase of aging on a positive note. Equally shining, both teach me how to be happy in the here and now. What this gives me is the world. And I admit, I like owning the world. Almost more than a new pair of shoes. And when I run out of real things to be anxious about—such as how I'm going to afford my health insurance or whether I should move my mom (who deals with aging on another, escalating level) next door or is Sequim close enough?— so that I go looking for something silly to fret over, like the inevitability of growing older, just ignore me. No matter how many columns it takes to work it through.

THE SILENT ISSUE
November 2005

Okay, I'm going to tell you a story that, tragically, will surprise no one. And though the script is not exclusive to Port Townsend and has been written before by many other artists in other desirable towns and cities, it's still an account from the front lines of an artist community and needs to be told again. Even if it makes some shake their heads thinking we creative types lack a fundamental understanding of economy no matter how much we choose to fight against it.

So, here goes: Each year, when the lease of my dance studio comes due, I confront my landlord. This sounds as if I wave my Italian hands around while he follows my gesticulations with his eyes, anger making me say stupid things. But it's not a showdown in that sense, more of a "plead for the arts" tete-a-tete, when the reality bomb drops and the fear of what another rent increase will do to my work life weighs down on me. And I don't plead solely for my dance company, as much as I need to, but for all working artists in this so-called artist community where most of us can no longer afford studio space inside the city limits.

Within the downtown building that houses my studio, I'm one of two, maybe three artists still hanging on. Over the last few years, most studios have turned "office" for banks, lawyers, corporations. I'm not saying these entities don't need a place to work just as I do, but I cling to the hope that more landlords will empathize with artists and adjust rents accordingly. Otherwise, there won't be an artist left working in the hub of our town. We'll disappear as fast as the sole proprietor of a video store. In fact, for the most part, we already have. As one artist friend put it, "I'm back to setting my easel on my kitchen table."

This isn't meant to say there aren't differences in degrees of hardship. There clearly are, affordable housing a more pressing issue. But, currently faced with how ineffectual my own denial can be, it's time for a reality-check (which is a better way of saying a "freak out"), because I've made the cardinal mistake renters often do, believing that the threshold over which I pass daily is mine and will remain so until I choose to move on.

Artists have always congregated in aesthetic, out-of-the way places so they can work in an environment that enhances what they do. Fast forward: The same place becomes a real estate mecca until its streets are more mediocre, more mainstream than before. Think Edmonds. Or Manhattan before lawyers eager for space that set them apart from the corporate feel of downtown, forced Soho artists to Jersey.

Words work their magic in a number of ways. Some weight has fallen off my shoulders, an easing of tension that comes from writing what I need to say. On a less personal note, I don't wish to assign blame but to help. Help by way of reminding our city's building owners to consider how artists helped to shape this community so that landlords now reap the benefits of that very shaping. I do realize owners have their expenses, too, but I wonder if being a landlord should ever be solely a business endeavor? Renting to people involves people, individual as they are, which takes a certain level of compassion.

We talk about art all the time in Port Townsend. But what does that mean, really, if working artists are run out of town? Leaving behind those who retire here with money in hand.

And our young artists? They need to leave town in order to imagine.

MAKING THE CUT

December 2005

This year, I'll face the month of December abiding by the words "less is more."

Despite umpteen years of over-optimizing the holidays, and over-spending and over-committing, I'm redefining the season on my own terms.

And though I question my ability to learn from past mistakes, fearing I possess the habit compulsion Freud wrote of, I like to think that when it comes to dealing with holiday pressures, I've gained a certain perspective over the years.

As a writer, I know how many words are nonessential, that the meaning of a story is not lost in the editing but more clearly revealed. I'll apply the same riddance to Christmas even when confronted with my family's expectations, as well as my own need to make life as creative as my work.

Here is a list of what I'll be cutting this year like unnecessary adverbs:

1. No TV. Not even "It's A Wonderful Life." Holiday programming inflicts a brutal nostalgia, worse than looking

through your high school yearbook. And I prefer my emotions moving forward. Especially this time of year.

2. No cookies. I'm not baking them, eating them, or accepting one cookie party invitation where I'm to bake a zillion just so I don't feel left out of an evening that bores me. No fudge either.

3. A simple wreath. A small tree. No other decorating. The thought of having to put up, take down, and pack away anything more drains my every cell of enthusiasm.

4. Visit my mother. Call my dad. It's not that he's a bad person. I just don't think, for a menagerie of reasons, that he and I are good family when we're together.

5. No card sending. If I had time, I'd handcraft them. But I don't.

6. Buy something special for a few people I love and let the store wrap them. No gifts for the B list. Somewhere along the way it became time to nix all that.

7. No feast of seven fishes. I still care about Italian tradition. Just not as much as I used to. Besides, anyone familiar with me knows I make a lousy Roman Catholic, so why work so hard at a biblical feast?

(Because I'm still trying to please my mother.)

8. Don't try to please my mother.

9. Make this a list of nine things rather than ten.

Add the extra minutes to my walk around the neighborhood where, after hours of writing about the past, I'm released into the exquisite and ordinary details of the present.

I KNEW IT ...

December 2005

At the movies, I sit next to a woman I have seen around town for years, a woman I've taken special note of because she reminds me of my mother. Which can elicit a feeling of undivided love and appreciation or something more equivalent to road rage, depending on the last conversation we had, or tried to.

While waiting for the film to begin, I go over and over in my head why this woman is so similar to my mom even though she has dyed red hair—instead of dyed blonde—and she wears an overabundance of silver jewelry rather than the gold accouterment my mother prefers.

Manner: the perfect word for why she and my mother resemble each other. Let's just say that if they shopped together, they'd be drawn to the same bric-a-brac. Or if they were to chat about the neighborhood, family, religion or politics—though they'd likely skip religion and politics—they'd agree about most things, or politely pretend to. They are mothers and grandmothers from the same era. And even if they have no more in common than having married and procreated in the fifties, they have lived through much of what life has to offer, good and bad, which becomes its own loyalty in the same way veterans bond over a shared war.

And if this month weren't about gift giving, which it *is*, I would be satisfied with a quick scan of how I feel about the woman sitting next to me. Then I'd lean back to enjoy the trailers. But tonight I am looking at her from the inside out, where the perspective is always more about listening than seeing. And if I listen carefully, it's not hard to hear why this woman has chosen a seat next to me.

Oh, God. I knew it. I *knew* it. What was I *thinking*?

You see, just yesterday I bought my mother's Christmas gift, the most exquisite 100 % silk blouse that will fall over her ... rather ample body and bosom in the most elegant way. But one glance at the woman beside me reminds how utterly inappropriate the gift is for my mother. The blouse is appropriate for, you guessed it, *me*. What my mother would enjoy receiving is a shirt similar to the one the woman beside me proudly wears: a red and green sweatshirt with the words "World's Greatest Grandmother" stitched in gold letters held up cheerfully by Mickey Mouse.

Let's back up. I need to back up here and say I have been trying to "remake" my mother most of my life.

And so if, at first, I didn't understand why this woman sat beside me tonight, I realize now that I know exactly why. To remind me to return the silk blouse. Tomorrow. First thing.

Because even though much of the sentiment of this month falls on my ears like a load of meaningless bunk, there is a real message here even for the most irreverent: Gift giving is about the person on the *receiving* end.

After the movie I will sit in front of my computer and Google "Disney Store." Because of all the people I need to buy for, mom is the one I most want to please.

Which I fully intend to do.

VII.

"*The remarkable thing is that we really love our neighbor as ourselves: we do unto others as we do unto ourselves. We hate others when we hate ourselves. We are tolerant toward others when we tolerate ourselves. We forgive others when we forgive ourselves. We are prone to sacrifice others when we are ready to sacrifice ourselves.*"

— Eric Hoffer

AS ONE SEASON ENDS
January 2006

As the new year settles in and thoughts of spring will be upon us any day now, naturally my thoughts turn to renewal. As always, there is much to consider.

There is nothing new for me to write about the sunlight's resurgence or, for that matter, the garden's. So I won't, other than to say I've already confronted every conceivable metaphorical image of seed within earth in previous writings, and the only thing I've come up with is that weather is too tedious to write about at all.

Intrinsically speaking, I feel another sort of season upon us. And should it not draw in soon, I'll be utterly disappointed in the way you are when you want and need something to happen and then realize it's not going to, *ever*. In the meantime, I fill in the gap with what it takes to move from one day to the next, the comforting routines of life: meaningful work, a marriage and friendships that fuse me solidly to life. Still, at what point do I face the fact, and I need to, that our country may not be up to receiving the season I am trying to describe?

In the last weeks, three separate (though connected) things occurred that pushed this very question forward for me. And though the word "illuminating" would be one way of describing the trio of events, "bruising" would be better because, one by one, each knocked me down to size. Which is a good place to be if there's any real change to be had, personally or politically.

One was that, on my commute from Bainbridge Island to Seattle, a Coast Guard vessel sped alongside our ferry, semi-automatic pointed at our bow. This is hardly a new phenomenon for commuters since Homeland Security set out to heal the past with fear of the future. But the gun seemed to typify such arrogance, such expensive arrogance, as it zig-zagged our starboard. Why in the wake of such needs as affordable housing and healthcare do we refuse to acknowledge that terrorism is not something we can target but something that spreads across our planet by those with little else to believe in? No weapon readied on the bow of a tag-along ship is going to remedy that.

And in this feeble attempt to reassure us, the show of force, instead, drove home the feeling that our ferry was under siege. Besides, it doesn't take brilliance to grasp that if terrorists can't get on board airplanes, they are going to find their way onto buses, subways (think London, Spain) and yes, ferries. So what does the Coast Guard hope to accomplish with weapons aimed at our ferry if not one of our bags was screened?

The second came about at airport security, where, of course, everything is screened. Ahead of me sat a man in a wheel-chair. That is, before two officers picked up his torso to run a baton underneath his legs or rather where his legs would be if he indeed had legs. The incident humiliated the man, horri-fied his wife, and terrified the onlookers. But the worst part, the part that made me cringe to where my husband had to hold on to me so I wouldn't go after the security crew, was how the same strong-armed men laughed as soon as the paraplegic rolled out of hearing range.

More recently, the third incident presented itself, making it possible, finally, for me to define this "season" I find difficult to name. While riding a city bus from downtown to Capitol Hill, I looked up to see a banner sign that read, "We're all in this together. If you see something or someone suspicious on this bus, call this number."

I'm embarrassed to say that at first I thought it was a prank, and I didn't take the words seriously. But when I did, they felt like a punch in my gut and it took me a while to loosen up again. For what, exactly, when it comes to the exotic mix of cultures, styles, and preferences that make up our country, especially our cities, defines "suspicious"? And who decides?

These are the questions I discuss at length with my new friend Geta, who drives a taxi. He was a teacher in Ethiopia. I befriended him because he is genuinely kind and interested in everything we converse about, and when he invited my husband and me to his family home, he was sincere.

It's not difficult to imagine his "suspicion" story: How, when he first arrived here, his dark skin and shabby clothes by American standards sent another in the underground bus terminal into tattling mode, dialing 911 on a cell phone without awareness of the many who escape civil war in Africa every day and who, if fortunate enough to have their names come up in a lottery that allows them to emigrate as did Geta, choose Seattle because of its rumored tolerance.

So what does all this have to do with a "season," you wonder? Well, only that it will take the kind of reclamation that can force bulbs to spring warm from the earth to turn this suspicion-schism around. We can either choose to recognize this "season" like noble people, or deny it with an ignorance that fear and false pride encourages. For the season I speak of is nearly tangible and can be described in one word: *forgiveness*. We have to find it within ourselves to forgive those few extremists who terrorized our nation by destroying two monuments in our greatest city. Forgive that they snatched from us our sense of security so that now we steal from ourselves every day by clinging to fear and implementing more and more surveillance tactics. We need to remember that the same fanatics stole from every moderate Muslim, which is the vast majority, a religion seeded in inquiry and tolerance. Forgive in the same way the Japanese people and the Vietnamese (and all the others) have forgiven us our terror-isms that once shook their nations.

Because it's our turn now. It's our season.

DEAD CENTER
March 2006

It is a March day in Port Townsend and I am walking up the Haller Fountain steps. The sky is sunless but it hardly matters. Anticipation lightens the air. And that's the best thing of all about March, that spring is nearly here, it buoys our temperament, beckons from above and below, promising relief, utterly and simply.

Suddenly, people who ignored me all winter are stopping on the sidewalk to chat, the waitress at the bakery is smiling, the postman is smiling, even the curmudgeon at the hardware store wears a grin, sort of. And you know and I know how that alone can make your day. It's as if everyone is taking stock and finding themselves wanting of each other again.

Maybe that's because, for many artists, it takes a certain self-assuredness, a head-down approach to our work when winter descends and we find ourselves zooming in on what it is we do. Which sounds wonderful. And mostly it is wonderful. But let me dispel the myth right now that it is anything even close to wonderful all the time. It's also solitary, bemusing, and frustrating as, say, waiting for a live voice to come on the phone when you ring up the airlines.

218

For me, the creative process steps up in Autumn, intensifies during winter, is there every morning when I awake and every night when I go to sleep, or try to. With so many dark hours to contend with, I scurry back to the warm, innermost sanctum of my office every chance I get even if what I meant to do is change the sheets I haven't thought about changing in weeks or make a meal other than popcorn and a salad. Well, not a salad *exactly*. More like lettuce straight from the bag.

To live in the Northwest in winter is to constantly consider what is most important to us. It's why the season is artistic process at its most exuberant as we connect to our work, and to ourselves, in a big way. And, at certain strategic times, such as before a deadline or performance, disconnect to anything or anyone other than what we need to get on the page, canvas or stage. "There is no substitute for hard work," Edison said. "And indeed, we go rotten without it."

And it's also why, come spring, it is really necessary to get outside of our offices and studios and, whew, out of our heads. A spring day can change everything and make of us, in more lighthearted ways, some new and terrific whole. Which has everything to do with connectedness. Actually, it's dead center.

So there you are. Although I hope this description doesn't sound too pompous to some: those who don't resonate well to art as anything but a touchy-feely hobby. Or to those who haven't yet tapped into their creativity but long to after working for decades in, suppose, an insurance office in Connecticut before moving here years after marriage and responsibility channeled their desires in a different direction.

Because it's hard for me not to mesh together life and pomposity while standing on The Haller Fountain steps—a staircase built long ago from wood with spacing that allowed Victorian gentlewomen to use it in ladylike fashion while hiking their hems to expose satin heels as they climbed to a prosperous summit.

And though that image is a far cry from my Puma sneakers and boot-cut jeans, I, too, am a woman ascending a bluff overlooking downtown, on the move in my own small world.

As for the ladylike fashion, well, no, I take the stairs two at time.

THE ART OF HARD WORK & THE HARD WORK OF ART

April 2006

Do you remember how you felt the first time you drove into Port Townsend? How, right from the start, you knew you were going to live here, self-determination rolling through you, what it takes to make a change rather than leave your life up to fate?

When you meet someone who recently moved to town, someone reveling in what I call the "honeymoon stage" of Port Townsend living, it's enviable. Especially if you've been here long enough to experience a few of a small town's down sides, such as those enemies you made without really trying, or the malaise that invades the psyche sometimes, a feeling akin to island fever.

There is no doubt envy is exactly what I felt when I met Eric Swangstu, a man who, in less than a year after moving here, transformed the lofts of The Old Alcohol Plant in Port Hadlock into The Art Mine, one of the finest galleries I've ever strolled through. But I welcome the kind of envy Eric nudges to the surface. It reminds me to stay true to myself so that I too remain enthusiastic.

Eric first came to Port Townsend to visit his mother-in-law, but it was more than family that prompted him to relocate. In our mid-thirties a new set of questions can arise that will drive our needs until we find new ways to attend to the future. Add becoming a father to the mix, and suddenly the dense, narrow streets of Manhattan's Hell's Kitchen didn't fit Eric's needs anymore.

I don't know how to talk formally about art, but I know attention to detail when I see it and I see it at The Art Mine. Within its gallery walls the drop-dead gorgeous steel plate flooring with little circle-etchings made me stand in silence with my mouth wide open.

"I squeegeed ketchup on it for the acidity," Eric told me. "Then I took an industrial grinder to it with my left hand so as not to control it too much. The result is interesting but it doesn't compete with the art."

You see, that's exactly the kind of attention I'm talking about.

But I'm not writing to inform you about Eric Swangstu. Instead, to answer for myself why I was compelled to write about him in the first place, likening it, I suppose, to my search for substance in life. To me, the real story of Eric has to do with what lies underneath his enthusiasm.

First, there's Eric's mother, an artist, who first showed him that life is, or should be, creative as a canvas. And Eric's father, a man who emotionally abandoned Eric at a young age. I suspect this made Eric's bonding with Paul Christensen, the owner of the inn where the gallery is housed, easier.

I also suspect that Paul Christensen, a resort magnate with no son of his own, sensed straightaway, as I did, that Eric is a man to be trusted. This father/son connection of younger-man-meets-older-entrepreneur is the best bonding hand-shake between men in the business world. And it's a rare thing these days.

Yet, if experience has taught me anything, there'll be some who turn envy of Eric's enthusiasm into, oh, an emotion more isolating than envy, and considerably less exemplary, a.k.a. jealously. Know why? It's easier then finding one's own passion. And it's part of the initiation a newcomer can expect if he takes the lead and sets his heights high and it can add up to a little bit of pressure.

Still, I bet Eric makes a success of The Art Mine in the same way he's made a success of life. Because he works hard at it. People forget that's what dreams are really built from: work. Good Lord, you can't wait for inspiration. That's a term used to avoid going to work. And you can't wait to be "discovered" or you'll likely wait forever.

Hard work, long hours—such as spending a week with a disc sander until a floor is no longer a floor but a creation.

CASTLE BUILDING

June 2006

One thing a longtime Port Townsend'er rarely talks about is what it's like to be one. If you know, what's to discuss? If you don't, it's not an easy thing to explain, especially within the limits of column space, but I'll give it a shot: If anything, the town is best defined as a community in the old-fashioned sense. Not a particularly imaginative definition, it's just one I haven't devoted time to explore as of late.

And by "old-fashioned" I don't mean "out of date," but rather that its size ensures that you will run into, say, your hairdresser at the grocery store, your dentist at the movies. You get the picture: living and working around the same people year after year; a family-like atmosphere with all the enormous frustrations and compatibility issues most families face.

One of the most liberating qualities I felt about Port Townsend when I first moved here from the East Coast was the lack of attention to status, the kind that floats competitiveness to the surface. Suddenly the college you attended, car you drove, or size of your home mattered little compared to the measure of your integrity.

In fact, I liked the freedom from caste so much, I bought my first home here. And, naturally, I asked all sorts of questions about the previous owner, Laretta Lafferty, a teacher who lived in the house half her life before a stroke caused her to fall to my very floor, where a neighbor found her. I don't know if being aware of this makes living in the house more meaningful, but it somehow restores my faith in neighborhood and accents the importance of continuum. Knowing whose life before mine dwelled within the four walls I now live in helps me appreciate history firsthand.

This is why I can't relate to the tear-down and castle-building mentality that's occurring more and more around town, actually around all of the country, as of late. Why would someone want to move to a community and then destroy the one thing that connects them to it? A revelation just occurred to me: Do these new homes need to be so big in order to house all the emptiness such a lack of connection to real things, things other than status, can bring?

My friend, Kathleen, who lives on U Street, told me a story all too familiar. Her new next door neighbor—from LA—informed Kathleen that she planned to tear down the house she'd just bought to build something that would "wow the neighborhood."

And just the other night I was having dinner with two actor friends who were excited that their local Key City Playhouse had recently purchased land to build a new theater. The only hangup for me was that in order to build the theater they would need to tear down the charming red cottage already on the Lawrence Street site. And given how the new artistic director of the theater only recently moved to Port Townsend, I doubt her roots go deep enough to care past satisfying desire, the wanting and re-wanting we believe will finally make us happy.

So I called the resident of the board of directors of the theater. And when he told me his first preference was to relocate the house, I thought, so much for that. I doubt it will happen, but bless him for trying.

I know what some of you are thinking: Americans should be able to do whatever they want with the land they buy. Please. I am so tired of this argument. And so tired of being tired of it. It reeks of self-centeredness. Which is fundamentally why so much of the world dislikes us these days, but, ahem, that's another topic altogether.

Or is it?

During the height of World War II, Hollywood produced its most elaborate mind-numbing musicals, fantasies that served Americans well. It's easier to cope with a love-gone-wrong scenario than what we really have to fear in the world.

Do you think this has any relevance to why, at this shaky point in time, we continue to build gigantic, castle-like houses and drive automobiles three, four times the size we need?

It's something to think about anyway.

Ah, but sociological patterns are cyclical. The eventual reaction is to seek the opposite. I find this a comfort, one that just might save Laretta's small home from the might of the wrecking ball when I'm no longer around to look after it for her.

INTO THE MOMENT

August 2006

Here it is, August already!

Huge to most of us who live here year round. Much ado. Every inch to be reveled in. Let the phone ring, emails pile up, it's recess! When life should be lived each moment. Not just on the weekend if and when you can carve out a little extra time.

For me that means draping myself in an Adirondack chair in my backyard, staring at my garden with parental pride, rather than sitting in my office, fused to my laptop, tending to every thought that flits around the edges of my mind (no matter how obsessed that sounds). No, this month is about a break in the page, the quiet within—even amidst all the organized merrymaking, the devised traditions our city is so good at promoting while I struggle to answer the most elemental question: Which festival, exactly, occurs this weekend?

And had I not overheard a woman say August is all about peace of mind because Mercury is no longer in retrograde, I might not have thought to write about how I feel about this warm-and-windless month that goes through me like dry champagne partly because it's all too rare in this oceanic convergence zone I call home. I have no idea what she meant, Mercury in or out of *any*thing feels like one new-ageism too many for me, even if it is a big celestial proactive thing or whatever. But from the look in her eyes, it's something good, and that's enough definition for me.

Oh man, there's just something about August, and I don't know if it's the way the light captures the treetops in the loudest golden silence or that it releases every generosity I feel for this place, the ones that get tucked up inside of me in, say, January, the month that makes me nuts, when my only saving grace is that I don't kill myself. Or is it a time-referential seed that gets planted in us at age six, a feeling of had-better-go-for-fun now before school starts and the season stiffens into fall? Whatever it is, I was born for it.

As was my friend Laura, who says in her energetic *kisskiss-gottagobye* style I adore, "It's about being outside in a tank top! When else can you ever be outside in a tank top?" Sun-lover that I am, I know just what she means, although anyone who knows us both will attest that said shirt is stunning on her curvaceousness and all but wasted on me even when unbuttoned down to here. But still.

By far the most gratifying part of this break in routine is time. For things like picnics. All year I long to grab my picnic basket (yeah right, okay, a blanket and some take-out) and head to the beach for dinner. Or to walk with a friend without the wind mowing us down as we amble over common ground: Work and gossip and family and films we love, and the wars and politics we hate. Floodgates open, no need to justify or defend what we say, real connection.

And not to go too lovey-dovey on you, but my friends and I, and I am sure of this, are exactly why those small bistro tables were invented, with only two chairs close enough so that a couple of girlfriends can lean into each other in confidence. Visually, this boils down to the components of what I love most about summer, or frankly, about life: It's all about good friends, good conversation, good food and drink, and laughter.

So pull up a chair. And be funny. Amuse me. And for Pete's sake don't mention fall. I feel sad for you if you are worrying that already.

LIKE THE CITY ITSELF
July 2006

Do you ever really get over a day like yesterday, Friday, July 28, 2006? Especially if you live and work in Belltown, Seattle?

I shrug and tell myself that of course I will, that the memory of six women shot at The Jewish Federation one block from where I live is a memory that will be drastically altered by the passing years, that life goes on, that like most everyone I know, I'm more or less desensitized to the images of violence that have bombarded my mind from every media angle all my life. I will accept no eloquent rebuttal to how this has affected my tolerance for horror and catastrophe.

Yet despite my self-consciousness in admitting this, or perhaps because of it, here I sit, lucky me, in the sanctuary of my tiny home, clicking away at my computer, sipping Spanish wine. All of which proves life does go on, and sometimes much too quickly.

Admittedly, if I were a 12-year-old I'd think nothing of the fact that one day after the fatal ambush, while our neighborhood still trembles on alert, the Torchlight Parade blares Cool & the Gang—*celebrate good times, come on*—one block east of the scene of the shootings, fans and suburban families from all over greater Seattle using the occasion to focus on just how loud they can cheer and sing along. From sidewalk fear to festivity in twenty four hours. It's enough to boggle even the most preoccupied mind. And it illustrates how removed from reality most Americans can live in the world right now.

I've been thinking a lot about this lately. How, no matter how attuned to the tragedies of the world, we in the United States are still able to compartmentalize our lives into distinct time segments, and once we finish watching or reading the news, we are able to carry on with our day, iPods inset as we tend to the details that give routine its proper weight as the coping mechanism we need.

But for the families of the six women shot by an ill and angry man opposed to the faith they practice, there are no such distractions left. And I regret that Seafair chose to march its floats and pirates down Fourth Avenue on the threshold of such a tragedy, giving our city no time to take pause or fully recognize the scale of what just happened over on Third.

And maybe that's why, like the city itself, or perhaps like the world's true colors, the parade this year seems a little shrouded in gray.

A fact, unfortunately, vivid enough to set this column into motion while I keep walking out on my balcony to watch the procession.

Watching as if there is anything I can do.

WIND, SAILS &
WEATHERED BOARDS

September 2006

Before you roll your eyes at another description of the Lavender Festival, you should know I don't live in Sequim or own a lavender field.

What makes me want to write about the festival now, more than a month after the event, is that in these last days of summer, as one planet submits to another, Port Townsend is about to host its largest annual festival which, in terms of traffic, is a tide that flows in and out.

I'm going to let you in on a little secret: I don't relate much to The Wooden Boat Festival. It makes me feel inept. I can't sail, sit on board, or walk the docks without getting queasy and feeling sort of wooden all over (pun intended).

This is very non-Port Townsend. And very not-saying-the-right-thing in certain social circles, but other than those who can afford to own and maintain a yacht, I find myself wondering where wooden boats belong in our future. That is unless the whole affair becomes too-sea-shanty-for-words. Which it has.

Perhaps I'd feel differently if it were the early 1900s.

Now lavender, dare I say, is more of a feminine celebration, thank you very much. It pays tribute to what rises from seed rather than from fallen timber and a whole lot of bottom paint.

And that's nothing compared with the way it feels to wrap my arms around the festival, literally. All that perfect purple is a purple you can drown in, its product more about appreciation than longing. To sit in a field of lavender while the Bush administration compiles a deliberately anti-environmental record … well, you gotta love that.

Still, festival-preference aside, no matter what Port Townsend celebrates, it's always a small town with huge heart. And about as far from the mainstream as many who long to leave convention behind are willing to go. And wooden boats are a vehicle to the very core of leaving convention behind, of leaving *every*thing behind, actually, and why so many of them stay tied to the dock 24/7.

And even if the boat festival is not my sort of fun, it's easy to celebrate the boatbuilders, men who build wooden hulls with Zen-like devotion. Take Ernie Baird, who named his sloop after his mother. He's a mindful man. As are most of these men. Of each other. Most definitely of boats.

Though, truth be told, I've watched more than a few of their marriages stagger and fall over the years because, and this is the stuff no one talks about at the festival, boats are way better at forgiving neglect than women are.

Men want wind, sails, and weathered boards. Or at least the fantasy of wind, sails, and weathered boards, especially when they remember the cubicle/office they return to come Monday.

Cha-ching! Enter festival economy.

Like I should talk.

I came away from Sequim with lavender cream, lavender shampoo, and quite intoxicated on lavender margaritas, *wahoo!*

So maybe there's really no difference between festivals if, in the end, they exist to tweak our fantasies by way of merchandising. And, as any true escapist knows, the best fantasies always stem from the unobtainable.

AT A LOSS

September 2006

Ah, I think, when I read Knute Berger's final "Mossback" column in *The Seattle Weekly*, which, by the way, has been my favorite alt-news column for years. Knute's brand of honesty is my weekly city-roundup fix. And I love my fixes. Giving up Mossback will be difficult, and there's no hard and fast detox for it, either.

Still, once you are a middle-aged columnist it is time to think twice about using words such as "slides downhill" when referring to the future of your home town. Else the source of the "frustration and alienation" you say you are feeling may be more obvious to your readers than to yourself.

Perhaps, and even if you are not letting on about such things, what you are experiencing is more of a personal downhill slide, when your waistline begins to infringe on territory that belongs to your hips, though I don't mean to imply this sliding is something that can be measured strictly in visible signs.

But anyone who's met Knute might have predicted the tone his last column would likely assume. For he is, and I mean no disrespect, the epitome of old-school Seattle. And not even the opportunity to give a few final words of hopefulness to a captivated audience could lift him past his lean toward pessimism, a trait I find in many who have grown up in Seattle and now must endure the city's growth spurts while they struggle to feel safe.

Maybe, in the long run, it's less painful to have a city like New York as a reference point, where the land was pulverized into the maximum per-capita square footage way before I was born and where one grows up to believe a city will never be anything other than noisy, intense, addicted, and problem-riddled.

Back there, in my old working-class neighborhood where men are clean shaven and smell of aftershave *always*, the sight of a Northwest "Mossback" on the sidewalk would likely raise some suspicions. But here he is an icon in a city that still admires a scraggly beard, especially when it fronts a brilliant mind. Which, in his case, I believe it does.

Still, exiting on a dire note about the future of Seattle is not a "humble" opinion, as the Mossback claims, for he has far too much influence for that. It is a curmudgeonly one, however, and maybe that's why he praises other curmudgeons in his closing paragraph instead of uplifting the city that granted him such columnist status in the first place.

And though I suspect I too would enjoy the curmudgeonly group Knute is now gratefully a part of, I'm still let down by the fact that he chose to leave us pessimistic about the fate of Seattle, which seems more like a personal sense of sliding down because, well, he is at a loss as to what else to do with it.

CALENDAR GIRL

October 2006

I've always thought of myself as a cat lover. Even as a kid, I was crazy about my cat.

So when Nancy Rudolph called me to ask if she could take my photograph—my *nude* photograph—for the 2007 Charity Cat Calendar, a project that supports Peninsula Friends of Animals, a nonprofit, no-kill shelter in Port Angeles, Washington, I agreed. After all, "Calendar Girls" is a favorite movie of mine, right? And any project willing to put real women up for viewing, naked or otherwise, ranks way up there with me and is always a welcome contrast to what takes place in the advertising world, where model's bums are no bigger than mine was at birth.

But it was more than that. All aflutter with flattery, not only did I want to believe the sensationally sincere lie that my forty-something-year-old body could be considered "calendar material," although of course that helps, I thought it would be a bit of spicy fun. I suppose I'll always be an ex-Catholic girl raring to sin a little, a perennial time lag between now and that monumental day when I truly feel like an adult.

You know how sometimes, naked in the bathroom, you pose in front of the mirror, take a look, take *another* look, and maybe do a little booty dance while trying to capture someone fun in the looking glass? Well, as the photo shoot drew nearer, I began looking a little too closely, trying to see myself as others would see me (okay, thighs a little dimply ... butt ... well ... ditto), attempting to lessen the chagrin by imploring myself to stand proud. Proud! *Humph*.

How many of us naturally have the body image that so public a display of nudity requires? Maybe it's another ex-catholic thing that embarrassment and nakedness are inherently entwined.

"I'm not embarrassed," I told my husband. "I'm just ..." He waited. I paused. "Embarrassed."

But when Nancy showed up at my door, along with another Nancy, the director of the shelter, Nancy Campbell, the full realization of what I was about to do hit me. I have a special set of coping tools for these moments: denial and denial. No problem. Ready set go. Inhibitions dropped along with my shawl!

To our delight, it was a fairy-tale fantasy photo shoot. Nancy and Nancy liked the photo. Relieved to giggles, I liked the photo. Which is rare. Most photos of *moi* cause my eyes to pop and my head to thrust forward while I try to figure out why my mother is staring back at me.

Then—and this was where everything about-faced—I emailed the very naked image to my trusted friend before ringing her up. "Well ..." is all she said in that way that is code for "ARE YOU INSANE?"

And when my husband looked at the image he laughed. Even a guffaw pushed its way out. Which surprised me. I certainly thought he deserved to die in that moment.

In a matter of hours my excitement went from lift-off to crash. I lay in bed staring at the ceiling, a nameless ache scraping my insides.

All the same, self-consciousness is no excuse for chickening out. Which I did. Sort of. And my lack of courage still haunts me.

Nancy was patient. Anyone who has the endurance to photograph a dozen women scuffling with ego would have to be. "We want you to be happy with the photo," she said. "And we want your husband to be happy too."

We met for a reshoot. A less-naked portrait ensued, and that's the photo of me that appears in the 2007 Charity Cat Calendar. Shawl strategically stationed. No major selling feature exposed. Sorry.

Of course, there are eleven other beautiful women uniquely posed in the calendar, their hidden gems obvious. And what are these hidden gems? Their hearts and minds, of course.

JUST IMAGINE
October 2006

As soon as I walk down Virginia Street, the question forms on my tongue like clockwork even before I reach the Pike Place Market: "Why, *why* do they allow cars to drive through the narrow street that fronts the market?"

Cars other than loading vehicles, that is.

Nine years ago, divesting myself of a car and whittling down possessions in order for my husband and me to move into a 480-square-foot Belltown condo was no easy feat. Part of what I wanted, other than to simplify, was to reclaim a walking lifestyle that included shopping at the Pike Place Market. Of all the things I wanted to change about my life, buying groceries from vendors rather than dealing with parking lots broad and routine as the aisles inside was way up there on my list.

So it's no surprise that I love Sundays at the market best, when the northern lane of Pike Place is roped off from car traffic so that strollers don't have to fear being run over by a taxi vying for time, and the street operates at a pace unhurried.

I suppose tolerating a visual blight of any kind when I can see it from a more aesthetic, albeit more romantic, perspective is not my forte. So when I see an engine-revving car/tank nearly half the size of my condo (and no more attractive and less practical today than it's ever been) trying to bully its way over cobblestone laid down in the early 1900s, well, I'm embarrassed to say it, but more than once I've addressed the situation with a remark that was just a little bit malicious— easy for an Italian girl who'd rather feel persuasive in the moment than wait for etiquette to dictate the pace of things.

The sad but inevitable conclusion is that, yes, the Pike Place Market is an American entity. Which means perpetuating the time-honored tradition of cars, cars, and more cars. This is what James Haydu, director of marketing & communications for the market, confirmed for me when he told me how the merchants who face the street have consistently assured him that "direct traffic access is important to their livelihood," which is cold comfort to those of us who walk through Pike Place on a regular basis. If the market merchants, like most of our society, continue to value automobiles over pedestrians, my guess, and my fear, is that many of us, especially during the summer months, will be walking to the new Whole Foods at Westlake & Denny.

What is incomprehensible to me is why we can't entertain a creative solution. Such as designating several car-free hours in midday when tourist flow is at a max. But, alas, James Haydu and I agree about the adage that seems to define Seattle as of late: That change, other than condo development, comes slowly to our city. And why this is so is still pretty unclear to me, even more than it was before, when it was already pretty ambiguous.

Still, if left to simple human inclination, I'm quite sure Mr Haydu would agree that a car-free market would improve the atmosphere for all. But reluctance to accept the responsibility for change is exacerbated in our litigious times. And taking the first step toward change involves risk. And fear of taking responsibility for a risk limits creativity in a myriad of ways every second of our lives.

Just imagine the Pike Place Market without a traffic crunch. I close my eyes and imagine it, remembering an open-air market in France where not a single automobile crowds through and where shopping does not feel like a rush-rush hassle but a social occasion. And Europe is our parent, wiser in many ways. We should not shrug off what our elder society can teach us.

I wish I could knock on every downtown dweller's door to ask people to help change our food shopping district into what it could be rather than the roadway it is.

But I can't take on this challenge just now. I have to follow-through on ones I've already set into motion.

What I can give is this column. Think of it as a rap at your door.

FORGIVENESS

October 2006

Originally I thought *As One Season Ends* was to be the final essay to this collection. It seemed to accent the thread that runs through the book. If anything, I think it felt big enough.

Then something inconceivable happened that moved my decision in another direction: In Lancaster County, Pennsylvania, a man ordered Amish boys and women to leave a one-room schoolhouse, tied up the girls and shot them, then himself, causing a hard silence to fall over our country. The kind of silence that promptly ripples into sound. Whenever we're jolted in this way, we are instantly more connected to ourselves. First we cry out. Then we need to talk. Even if we struggle and don't know what to say. And some of us can't write fast enough.

It is a tragedy that could begin a book, really, if I only had the strength and the will, the tenacity and nerves of steel to tell a story that begins with death and ends with ... I want to say *life*. But I can't. It would be wishful at a time when wishing seems ludicrous. So many school shootings and no real change in gun control laws? It's enough to make me suspect of popular opinion forever.

Nevertheless, here is how I imagine it, how I might begin retelling the story: with an image of children sitting at wooden desks in a schoolroom, a horse-driven cart meandering by against a field in the background, two women working at sewing machines in a house nearby.

But I don't want to recount the story of the Amish tragedy. We already know more about the Amish people and the gunman than we need to in order to fully understand when someone loses his grip on sanity and then carries out another rampage shooting. It could have been anyone's children. The fact that it was one of the most defenseless schools in our society, where kids are unaware of most of the world's evils beyond its borders, makes the whole incident beyond imagining — if only we didn't need to.

Still, what is even more fearsome for me to read is that the predominant pattern in school and other premeditated shootings over the past three decades is this: Girls are the majority of victims. Here is when the recent shootings in my own neighborhood come back to me in a gruesome flash, the women shot at The Jewish Federation in Seattle. Also when my thoughts begin to slowly darken until—within hours of reading this piece of information—they grow completely black.

So because I live by the sea I start walking toward it, and then I run as if only the beach can offer sanctuary. Then I stop running, walk for a while, and start back. The tide comes in, waves rush against the waterfront. I vow to relax, to try to feel less edgy about the world, and to let the whole tragic Amish story go.

But today I think even more about the story, how if I were to write it as I see it, I would need to circle back to what frustrates me most, the confusion I feel about what it means to be female in a world where most assaults are carried out by men. How, as young girls, we are shown image after image of a male god who is supposedly at the center of all that is good and knowing, and yet, what we see are men at the center of things harmfully aggressive.

What is happening to me is reasonably clear: Tragedy is important as a subject of interpretation, much as religion is, or should be, much as life itself. And it's why I would need to turn around and speak to the past in order to find some glimmer of recognition about the present phenomenon of men killing girls that one of my friends likened to hunters shooting doves.

It didn't occur to me when I started writing this essay that I'd begin to think so much about how this underlying confusion of being shown one truth and experiencing the opposite gives so many girls a lack of esteem from the very beginning and why orders like the Amish arise in the first place. Where fathers, husbands, grandfathers, and brothers have the last word. Always. Where each Amish congregation is served by a bishop, two ministers, and a deacon. All male. Whether we are talking gender, race, religion or even a gunman, how easy it is to bully those set up to be fundamentally inferior.

Which makes me question how we can view the Amish any differently from other male-dominated orders anywhere. Even if what we'd rather do, because right now we feel the Amish loss so explicitly, is hold dear the fairy-tale illusion of their order as peacefully contented. Because how peaceful, really, can life be for a woman unallowed to be other than passive? Where does will and desire manifest if allowed only to ferment within?

I hear people say all the time that this is simply the way of the world. My mother loves to recite this. Also, "It's in God's hands." Pretty much her favorite wrap-up to any conversation demanding too much introspection. But my mother is just one of millions willing to hold on to all kinds of comfy illusions and certitudes rather than think, or worse, talk, about things too near the truth. Even with all of our American advances, we are still living in a time, unfortunately, when both sexes in most of the world accept over-simplifications for why, when it comes to politics and professions, men are center stage most of the time.

When I read that the mothers of the girls, or any women for that matter, were not in the room when the decision was made to raze the schoolhouse where the girls died, I wanted to scream. For one thing, the decision seemed far too hasty for an order whose daily lives are like time standing still in comparison to ours. But it is not unlike a shunning, really, a custom the Amish practice—an erasure of what is true. Because I also read that, and this will not surprise, it is the Amish elder men who will strictly enforce a shunning, when mothers and sisters cannot comply. So it's not that I don't understand why they don't allow women to be a part of the final words; I understand all too well.

I'm not suggesting the women should run things but that there needs to be a balance. I wonder, if the mothers had been present behind those closed doors, if they would want to rinse off the schoolhouse so quickly. As anyone who has been through something tragic knows, confronting the schoolhouse could allow for healing. Tearing down the school is escape. A bare and vacant field offers nothing but a bare and vacant memory. Healing is a somber, shadowy, and very slow process.

But how many men do you know, really, who are able to deal with their emotions directly?

Of course we are all at fault here for not allowing our men, especially our leaders, to appear humanly connected to realities such as vulnerability and the overflows of emotion that most women allow to run through them, sometimes on a daily basis. Most men will deny these spillovers at any cost. It's why rage collects. And explodes. And in the worst-case scenario, the explosion is a gunman with a grievance.

If all this seems like an unreasonable connection to the Amish story, a wacky turn, well, writing is a mysterious thing and it tends to open the very doors I set out to close. So I need to mention this false perception of the Amish not because I wish to be cruel at a time when the Amish deserve nothing but peaceful healing or because I dislike men. I don't. My point is not as simple as that. I need to mention all of this because I believe somewhere within all of this mystery is the very explanation I seek as to how a man, a husband, a *father* could walk into a room, let the boys go, and then shoot a room full of little girls no matter what past obsession he suffered from.

All of this makes me appreciate how long the process of paying tribute to the World Trade Center is taking. Even if we also come around to leaving the site void of anything but memory, it's not a bad thing to take our time. For I've stood over that horrific hole in the ground. It hardly needs embellishment to enlighten grief. Process takes awhile. And the result is more deeply gratifying than a quick fix.

Mercifully, there is something positive for me to add about Amish tradition. Their wanting to forgive the man who executed their daughters in the hope that the absolution would hasten their healing is a glistening example for the world. The humility of such forgiveness is surprising at first, as startling as being awoken at night by a clashing sound. Such pardon would be something good for our world leaders to strive for. Even if we know by experience that wanting something doesn't make it true, seeking forgiveness is a quest worth pursuing. Imagine our world if governments could be as yielding.

It's not unexpected how this tragedy has forced the Amish into my thoughts way too much. Regrettably though, it has taken my focus off the girls who lost their precious lives. I admit this is how I cope: I confront the big picture when reality is still too hard to write or even think about. Especially every single time I recall that the little girls' wrists were bound.

Fear, history teaches us, has the potential to immobilize an otherwise well-meaning public. It's what religion and regimes rely on. And just in case you don't think you did anything bad enough to fear hell, there is always Original Sin.

And that is why it is easier for me to understand our evangelical president these days. He cannot, in his pious mind, separate the way he governs from the way he preaches. Fear is his point of reference. I say this because I'm quite sure that if the gunman in Lancaster, Pennsylvania, had used his pent-up rage to shoot people in a location thought to be a "political" threat, our government would exploit it to preserve its intentions. And because this very kind of exploitation is how this collection of essays began, I feel it appropriate to come full circle and say it is also how it will end.

AUTHOR'S AFTERTHOUGHTS:

It's as if while compiling and rewriting this collection I lost myself. And so, paradoxically, I found my way home. And it has nothing to do with the region I live, though I don't belittle how important a sense of place is to a writer, to anyone. But it's taken me years and years to accept the fact that I don't really have two lives; my life and my work are one. Together they are the quiet inside that grounds me.

Aside from this discovery, huge to me, I learned that I don't need to answer all of the questions that can haunt me, I just need to keep asking them by way of writing. And I don't have to know where my writing is headed. I just need to know where it's headed *tomorrow*. Accepting this engenders doing the work one step at a time. And so I become.

And finally, that it's important to write one, maybe two "lighter" pieces after I spend days addressing a dispiriting, world issue. The "big picture" is an exhausting challenge.

These insights might sound a little too how-to, but they offer respite from the anxiousness writing can bring about as, one day after another, I fall freely into my work in order to land my take on the world.

I might not have intended to right myself by writing this book, but mind to page, I did.

ABOUT THE AUTHOR

Sanelli works as a writer, public speaker, columnist, and radio commentator.

She is a regular columnist for *Art Access*, *The Peninsula Daily News*, *The Queen Anne News*, *Peninsula Woman's Outdoor Magazine*, *The Belltown Messenger*, and *Peninsula Lifestyle Magazine*. She also contributes periodically to *The Seattle Times*.

Her commentaries have been aired on Weekend Edition, NPR, as well as on KSER FM, KONP AM, and KBCS FM. In 2001 & 2002 she was a regular commentator on WEEKDAY: KUOW: Northwest Public Radio.

She is the author of six poetry collections. Her poetry has been published widely and was recently included in two anthologies of Western Women Writers published by Houghton Mifflin. Her latest collection, *Craving Water, Poems of Ordinary Life In A Northwest Village*, is an intimate glimpse of life in the Northwest. Her collection *Close At Hand* was chosen as one of nine Northwest titles in 2005 to be put into Braille by The Seattle Public Talking Book Library. Her newest collection, *Small Talk*, is forthcoming from High Plains Press in 2008.

She divides her time (and psyche) between Belltown, Seattle, and Port Townsend, Washington giving her commentaries, books, and columns both an urban perspective and a small-community intimacy simultaneously.

This is her first collection of essays.

Aequitas Books is a new imprint of *Pleasure Boat Studio* which focuses on nonfiction books with philosophical or sociological themes. **Falling Awake** is the third book published under this imprint. Following is a complete list of books by *Pleasure Boat Studio: A Literary Press:*

Monique Luisa Coelho Translated from Portuguese by Dolores DeLuise and Maria do Carmo de Vasconcelos

Way Out There: Lyrical Essays Michael Daley

The Case of Emily V. Keith Oatley

Against Romance Michael Blumenthal

Speak to the Mountain: The Tommie Waites Story Dr. Bessie Blake

Artrage Everett Aison

Days We Would Rather Know Michael Blumenthal

Puget Sound: 15 Stories C. C. Long

Homicide My Own Anne Argula

Craving Water Mary Lou Sanelli

When the Tiger Weeps Mike O'Connor

Wagner, Descending: The Wrath of the Salmon Queen Irving Warner

Concentricity Sheila E. Murphy

Schilling, from a study in lost time Terrell Guillory

Rumours: A Memoir of a British POW in WWII Chas Mayhead

The Immigrant's Table Mary Lou Sanelli

The Enduring Vision of Norman Mailer Dr. Barry H. Leeds

Women in the Garden Mary Lou Sanelli

Pronoun Music Richard Cohen

If You Were With Me Everything Would Be All Right Ken Harvey

The 8th Day of the Week Al Kessler

Another Life, and Other Stories Edwin Weihe

Saying the Necessary Edward Harkness

Nature Lovers Charles Potts

In Memory of Hawks, & Other Stories from Alaska Irving Warner

The Politics of My Heart William Slaughter

The Rape Poems Frances Driscoll

When History Enters the House: Essays from Central Europe Michael Blumenthal

Setting Out: The Education of Li-li Tung Nien Translated from Chinese by Mike O'Connor

To see a list of our Chapbook Series and Backlist contact our website
www.pleasureboatstudio.com

Pleasure Boat Studio: A Literary Press
201 West 89th Street
New York, NY 10024
Tel: 212-362-8563 / Fax: 888-810-5308 / Email: pleasboat@nyc.rr.com